Ready? Sex? Wait!

Vivian Elebiyo Okojie

ELEVIV PUBLISHING GROUP
HOUSTON, TEXAS 77082

Ready? Sex? Wait!
By Vivian Elebiyo Okojie

Some of the stories in this book are pure fiction and are just examples. Not all of them are based on specific people or occurrences. Any character similarities are pure coincidence. Some sections of this book illustrate my own personal stories and I have used fictitious names for those involved

Ready? Sex? Wait! credits:
Book Layout & Art Direction: Nestto Graphics
Cover Design: Nestto Graphics
Photographer: Vincent Aziza

Published by Eleviv Publishing Group
Houston, TX 77082, USA
www.elevivpublishinggroup.com
1-713-548-3184

ISBN: 978-0-9886289-4-6

Scripture quotations are taken from the HOLY BIBLE, NEW INTERNATIONAL VERSION®. NIV®. Copyright © 1973, 1978, 1984 by International Bible Society.

Copyright © 2011 by Vivian Elebiyo Okojie
All rights reserved. No part of this publication may be reproduced or distributed in any form or by any means, or stored in a database or retrieval system, without the prior written permission of the publisher.

Printed in the United States of America

Dedication

To my beloved husband, Ehimare:
You are the expression of God's love for me.

To my lovely sons:
Eric and Edward

To my parents:
Chief & Mrs. Elebiyo

To my wonderful sisters and brother:
Toyin, Taiye, Kehinde, Maria and Mayowa

Acknowledgments

There are many people I would love to extend my gratitude to for all their support in making this book a reality.

First, to God almighty, without whom I am nothing.

To my sweetheart, Gibson Ehimare Okojie, my baby, you have been my rock and support. Thank you for everything. I love you.

To my sons, Eric & Edward, mommy is living her dreams, I pray you live yours too. I pray for your purity everyday and pray that the world would not ensnare or change who you are. I love you both.

To my parents, Chief & Mrs. Elebiyo, for all your love. Thank you for believing in me and instilling in me the importance of hard work and the pursuit of dreams. I love you.

To my spiritual parents, Pastor & Mrs. Sanusi, you have taught me service, holiness, and meekness. Thank you.

To Daddy G.O., you have been a beacon of light and, as I follow Christ, I look at you. Thank you for your prayers.

To my siblings, Kehinde Daramola, Toyin, Taiye, Maria, and Mayowa Elebiyo. You are great. I love you all.

To my cousin, Lekan Olowo and my aunt, Mrs. Dele Olowo, thank you so much for everything.

Acknowledgments

To Late Mr. Kelvin Emordi, I love you and I miss you, Uncle K, trying to run fast like you, you have left a gap in our hearts no one can fill.

To Mrs. Pat Emordi Akugha, I love you past the moon; you are the strongest woman I know. I learn from you each day. Keep singing. I love you.

To Mr. & Mrs. Okojie (Uncle P & Sister Joyce), I thank you for your support. I love you both.

To the Akughas, and Emordi family in Houston, Texas. I love you guys.

To Mrs. Shola Ipinmoroti, thanks for your support while making changes to this book. You are awesome!

To Mrs. Olakitan Akinbamiro, thank you for pushing me to get this book printed.

To my very good friend, Mrs. Busayo Fasidi, I love sharing ideas with you, and laughing with you. To Mr. Fasidi (Bishop) thank you for always telling me to slow down.

To Dr. & Mrs. Ojifini, thank you for your support.

To the youth group at RCCG Restoration Chapel, Houston, Texas. I love you guys.

To Pastor Timi Owobo-Judah, for coming up with a great book cover; it's been awesome working with you. You are truly an amazing person!

To Diane Tezeno, thanks for editing my work and always available to help out. Thank You.

To Kathy Bennett, thanks for doing all it takes to edit my work. You are the best book doctor ever. Springfield was a blast!

To Tina Amadi, thanks for your ideas, and friendship.

When I look at you, I see a God given strength- don't know how you do it!

To members of The Redeemed Christian Church of God worldwide, it is an honor to be a part of this great church.

To all those who contributed stories to this book, your words will reach millions and thank you.

To all those who are in search of the true meaning of purity and to those living in purity.

To everyone I forgot to mention, I love you all.

CONTENTS

Dedication	iii
Acknowledgments	iv
Commentaries	ix
Foreword	11

READY? — 13

Chapter 1: Ready? Set? Go!	16
Chapter 2: Lessons I Learned About Sex	24
Chapter 3: Are You Ready?	50

SEX? — 53

Chapter 4: Sex, Sex, Sex: Going Out To Making Out, Hooking Up To Breaking Up	56
Chapter 5: Sex, Virginity, And What?	62
Chapter 6: Sex, ETC.	70

WAIT! — 93

Chapter 7: Waiting Sucks, But The Wedding Night Is Awesome!	96
Chapter 8: Who Are You Dating?	102
Chapter 9: Keeping Yourself Pure	114
Chapter 10: Stories I Heard Or Were Sent To Me Over The Years	128
Workbook	154
Glossary	165

Commentaries

Ready? Sex? Wait! offers a frank, down-to-earth look at sex and equips teens and those seeking to reclaim their abstinence with valuable tools and insights that will aid them in safeguarding their bodies and spirits. Elebiyo's transparency in sharing the missteps she made on her own personal journey makes this a must-read for young people looking for practical advice and guidance. I recommend this book to schools, ministries and youth groups that are looking for a spiritually-based way to encourage women, young and old, to safeguard their most precious God-given gift.

~ **Diane Tezeno**

Ready? Sex? Wait! couldn't have come at a better time in our world where all manners of sexual improprieties, immoral suggestions and exploitations have become the order of the day, while leaving many young adults confused and disoriented in the process. We live in a time and age where chastity is unfashionable and virginity is a taboo. Many of our young people today are under so much sexual pressure from their peers, the media, the fashion and entertainment industries, some of the books they read, some aspects of their academic curriculum, and in some cases, even their parents. As a father of three beautiful daughters myself, I welcome this timely material and highly recommend it for every young woman and their parents who still believe in the virtues of chastity and purity.

~ **Timi Owobo-Judah**

I really enjoyed reading this book. I am sure it will be an excellent read for teenage girls, their parents and guardian. It is an honest rendering of what people go through as teenagers. I really like the part about stories from people's past experiences. We need more people to pen down their past experiences so that the coming generation can learn from the successes and otherwise of others. It takes boldness and Vivian has done that.

~ **Dr. Rotimi Ojifini**

Foreword

What you learn and the way you were brought up as a child can greatly impact your life positively or negatively. For this, one must commend the efforts of Chief & Mrs. Elebiyo for a good upbringing. The bible says, "Train up a child in the way he should go: and when he is old, he will not depart from it. (see Proverbs 22:6 KJV) Though she did not know it all the author, as a youth, kept to what she knew and that helped her a great deal.

Today sex is being exploited by the devil whose major objective is to derail people from their divine destinies. Sex was designed by God for the expression of love between a man and his wife as well as for procreation; not to fulfill carnal lusts. It is not to be bastardized, exploited or used to turn mankind, made in the image of God, into dogs. Sex is good and only allowed within the confines of marital relationships (see Hebrews 13:4).

Satan, the enemy of man, is aggressively exploiting sex to destroy the lives of many young people today. Even adults too are not excluded from the abusive and destructive power of illicit sex. The Bible tells us in Proverbs 6:25 that, "… by means of a whorish woman a man is brought to a piece of bread: and the adulteress will hunt for the precious life" (KJV).

Unfortunately, sex education is not being properly taught to children by their parents and educational institutions. Rather, these children are left to discover and learn about it themselves and this is done, more often than not, in the wrong way, especially through the media. The bible says, "Stolen waters are sweet, and bread eaten in secret is pleasant" (Proverbs 9:17, KJV). When a child reaches the age of puberty, the tendency is for him or her to want to explore the secret that is being hidden from him or her. That is why parents must take time to be bold enough to educate their children about sex so that they will not be misinformed.

This book will be an excellent read for both adults and youths. They will help the youth to avoid mistakes that are sometimes difficult to correct and often lead to perpetual regret. Many of our young people can avoid this pitfall if they'll learn from the experiences of the author who is so frank and kind enough to share this timeless information with the coming generation. Some adults also need to remember that there is no joy in sex outside of marriage. It is nothing but a deceit of the devil. *Ready, Sex, Wait!* counsels you to look before you leap.

Have understanding and do not destroy yourself with sex outside of marriage. It's not worth it. The wedding bed is sweet and glorious. Wait for it.

Pastor K.B. Sanusi

Ready?

Premarital sex also known as youthful sex and young-adult sex is sexual activity, including vaginal intercourse, oral sex, and anal sex, practiced by persons who are unmarried.

Historically considered taboo by many cultures and considered a sin by numerous religions, it has become more commonly accepted in the last few decades.

Has our generation become more accommodating of sex outside of marriage?

"With my thighs ajar, here's a basket of love,
Take refuge my prince, my purity awaits,
This moment you'll have me untainted by touch,
For burden of birth, owe mother this much."
— Amatielle Silva

CHAPTER 1
Ready? Set? Go!

My struggles with lust started at a very young age. In elementary school, I would tilt my head enough for a little boy to notice my lips. I learned this from watching my auntie flirt with men. I was fascinated by her and the attention she received and I thought she was beautiful and fun to be around. Surely, it was a good thing to do to draw attention to my lips. It was a good thing to do because my auntie did the same thing. The excitement in her mannerisms when men noticed her lips and hair drew me like a moth to the flame. I wanted that excitement and sophistication in my life. I mimicked her and I tilted my head like she did because, sometimes, the little boys would look at my lips too.

In middle school, I wanted to kiss someone very badly. Kissing sounded so magical. Fairy tales ended with a kiss and then there was happily ever after. The first kiss of true love bound lovers together forever. I thought about kissing, wondering about the way it must feel, the way I would feel, and the powerful magical binding of hearts I thought would happen as soon as I kissed the right boy. Secretly, I practiced kissing my hand, watching myself in the mirror to see if I might be doing it correctly.

In high school, I wanted nothing more than a guy's appreciation for my body. I desired the appreciative looks that I saw in the eyes of boys I encountered. It made me feel powerful and alive to have heads turn. I dressed carefully every day, showing my body to its best advantage. I wanted to especially attract the best and strongest men. I wanted to be the center of attention because of my beauty.

In college, I wanted sex in some manner. I wanted in some way to have the unexplained explained to me. I wanted to know what the buzz about sex was all about. My body ached to be loved and I found myself responding to the false intentions of the men I knew, but I was lost in wanting. College opened my eyes to a whole new feeling of sexuality. The possibilities were endless for a girl like me who was innocent and who knew very little about the mechanics of sex. I discovered there were many men who were eager to teach me what I had never imagined, I was dumbfounded but excited. I thought I could have my pleasure without any consequences. The majority of my friends in college had sex. The stories of weekend escapades and nightly encounters made my mouth water. I wanted it too.

I wanted it, but I feared it. It broke my heart when I thought about my precious friends giving away their virginity on dirty little couches, smelly twin beds, and the back seats of cars. Where was the romance? When I heard guys talking about doing it in the car, in bathrooms, behind dorm rooms, and in movie theaters, my spirit shriveled inside of me. How could this be honorable? The things I heard guys say about their sexual partners were devastating to me and I was ashamed that, perhaps, someone was saying those things about me.

To say the least, these experiences were not appealing to me. I was a bit too traditional. I wanted my first time to be in a big, king-sized bed with rose petals scattered on the bed sheets. I wanted to kneel beside my bed with the song of my heart kneeling beside me and be thankful for the sweetness of love. I wanted to join my husband in a holy union, a glorious joining of two flesh becoming. I wanted his respect and passion to be pure and strong. I wanted breakfast in bed or, even better, the knowledge that we would share breakfast every morning at our own table with our wedding rings shining on our fingers.

I wanted my first time to be special. I wanted the guy to stay for another sixty or seventy years. I wanted to have kids as a result of our union. I wanted a real life together like the one my parents shared. But, as badly as I wanted that, I also just wanted to get it over with. I wanted to be on my way and to have intimacy be a normal part of my existence. I was torn between what I wanted and what I desired. I would try to stop my memories because they became tinted with flashes of lovemaking that I had watched and picked up on television. I would lie awake at night thinking of redeeming myself from my flesh. I would agonize over the truth that I am only human despite all my attempts to play the saint of chastity. I am only a hypocrite who deceived my dates into thinking that I did not want it as much as they did.

My facade was my starry-eyed innocence and my ability to say no. But I wanted it too. I wanted that one thing that was forbidden until marriage. I wanted to explore. I am only human and I wanted the same thing that six billion other people in the world want—that thing we call love.

I lamented the fact that I was probably the only virgin left on earth. Every time I looked around, everyone and everything was dripping with sex. I used to wonder what the big deal was about sex until I turned 18 and I realized that people my age were already sexually active. To say the least, I used to wonder why I was different, but, by the time I turned 19, I found out that I could not run away from society's pressures. After a few of my late night dates, I engaged in what is commonly called necking, some kissing, and you know the rest.

I never was one who felt the need to follow the crowd, but, in my own little way, I really did. I thought nothing was wrong with a little necking here and there, or some illusion of intercourse like dry humping. Back then, a lot of guys my age only wanted to "pop the cherry" and then leave you hanging. I was not ready for such an emotional roller coaster or the disappearing act the guys pulled once they "got some." Although I was not ready for the drama that developed from giving myself away tiny little pieces at time. Through all my dating experiences and everything that happened between the men that I dated, I never had intercourse with them. Therefore, I claimed that I was a virgin. But I was not. In my head, which contains the most real events of my life stored in memory as well as my perceptions and concepts that propel me through my life, I had consummated dozens of relationships and made love countless times through the aching darkness of aloneness in the night.

In the physical reality of my life, I had fallen short of His glory. There was just one thing I did not know but which is now clear to me. Giving myself away in bits had robbed me of the pure experience God intended for me. I was not as innocent as I thought because, I am too aware of my past.

The truth is that once you have gotten sexually involved with a man and you have either practiced oral sex, and everything in-between, then you can no longer be considered a virgin. You cannot say you are abstaining from sexual intercourse but be engaging in everything else. Talk frankly to older women who have been married and have had children and they can clarify that sex is sex and intercourse is just one part of sex. If this is true, then who has hope of living a pure life? Can it be that the only young women who can be called pure are the ones that live sequestered and sheltered with their every move monitored and tested by the authorities in their lives? Never believe that!

As I dredged through my past, I saw how, despite all my imperfections, God's love was still evident in my life. I was not one that led a wild life, but I did go out with the wrong men. It is funny because, all that time, I professed to be a virgin. My mind kept telling me that, as long as I was not having intercourse, it was alright. But I was deceiving myself. I have always been an advocate of purity and chastity publicly though I never followed it truly myself.

The truth is that no one is perfect. You make mistakes, you learn, and you move on.

You can leave your past behind, guarding your present, including its desires, and leaving your future to God who, in due time, will bring you to your spouse whole and without blemish. I noticed over the years as I speak to young people across the country that it is easy for us to tell young people to stay pure, but sexual desires are always present. The question is how do we keep our purity? We have to tell young people how to handle temptations, how to say no, and what to do when resistance fails. Looking back at my life and dating experiences, I feel bad for all the things I did. However, I choose to move forward. It is okay to feel a sense of guilt, but it is not okay to feel condemned. Ask for forgiveness and move on. Flee from those things that easily tempt you. Spend time learning about keeping your mind pure. Begin to reclaim your body through God. Ask him to restore your body back to you so that, on your wedding night, it will feel like the first time or as if you have never been touched. Reclaim your gift of purity.

To be pure, to remain pure, can only come at a price, the price of knowing God and loving Him enough to do His will.
He will always give us the strength we need to keep purity as something as beautiful for Him."
— Blessed Mother Teresa

CHAPTER 2
Lessons I Learned About Sex

Our ideas of sex are shaped by our culture and background. What I learned as a little girl somehow imparted in me, the values I still hold dearly. What has shaped your belief system? Who taught you about sex? The question is how much impact those factors have on your ideals about men, dating, marriage, and sex. I wrote this book, as a single woman in the quest for the love of a man and passion that comes as a result of that love; but realizing after marriage that loving oneself is the most essential necessity as you navigate through the trenches of singleness. What factors really shaped my ideas about sex; and what shaped my attitudes towards men? Why the innate curiosity about sex, and how my curiosity had shaped my actions and consequently my divine revelation?

As I think back to times with my friends. There is not much that goes on in a small town, especially during the holidays. Christmas was fast approaching with the jingle bells, sleigh bells, and shining Christmas lights. We drove around in circles chattering and catching up and, as always, our discussion went on for hours as we talked about everything, "men and sex." We took a trip down memory lane, thinking about all the men we have dated or wish we dated.

You see, my girlfriend and I had pledged allegiance to the Virgin Club long before our first dates at the age of 14 and, ten years later, we were beginning to wonder if it was worth it. We laughed and got mad as we called out names of boys who disappeared because we decided not to have sex with them. It was midnight when I got home. I slipped on something comfortable and went to bed. My phone rang and my friend, Charity, was on the line. Her voice was full of pain. Her sister was pregnant and not married, and Charity's heart was breaking for her. I listened and I ached with her because of her sister's troubles. Charity had come a very long way in her quest for purity, and she understood, better than most, the pitfalls of losing oneself in a moment of lust and forgetfulness. After we got off the phone, I went to my desk and took out an essay that I had written about my struggles. It summed up my journey to understand myself better. I sat down and read it again...

Everyone can remember the first time they fell in love and the feelings that somehow shaped our existence and attitudes—to feel the warm fuzzy feelings of one's first love and believe that their new love was the greatest of all things. The innocence of that feeling, the feeling that the new love will last forever, the tingling sensation; then the flopping wings of a thousand butterflies in the pit of your stomach; when you would feel the starry eyed innocence of your first love. For some, it was the best time in their lives and, for some, it was the worst: the first kiss, first love letter, and, for some, the first time they had sex or at least wished they had or had not. I found love in my English class in eighth grade. We were to write letters to someone in a nearby town as a part of our lessons on letter-writing. I was given a boy to write to and, at first, I was embarrassed, but soon I was thrilled. His name was Kenneth and his letters were breathtaking. Very soon thoughts of what he was like and the beautiful things he said filled my mind and he was the center of my day. I imagined and wished above all else that he would hold me when and if we eventually met. After several months of writing, we were finally able to meet.

It was magical. We were so innocent and full of words to share. We talked about everything and nothing during our brief time together. I could not imagine anything being better than to just be with him, walking in the warm sunshine with our hands occasionally brushing against each other. Far too soon, it was time for us to go. In the shade of a spreading tree, Kenneth took me into his arms and embraced me. We held each other close like in the movies. I closed my eyes and tilted my head just enough. He moved so close I could hear his heartbeat. It was perfect, sweet, and innocent. The memory of that day fills my heart with happiness even now after all this time.

That was the first and last time I ever saw Kenneth. We were children, really, and our lives and hearts quickly moved on. My heart never wished I slept with him. Once in a while, he runs across my mind and I think about how been with him was such a big deal for me then and how I left town to go to another state just to see him. How I wish all of my experiences were so innocent. Now, times have changed and I have bigger demons to deal with—the cravings that bring about discontentment as well as the choice between my sexuality or sexual cravings and my spirituality. So many of my prayers are geared towards purity and fleeing youthful lust and desires that I, sometimes, do not have time to pray for the world. I am filled with outrage and disgust at myself, and my prayers are full of grief for my lost innocence.

I plead with God, "You just have to heal me now and deliver me from this bondage or else." After that, I do not know what to pray after that. I am not an addict who has to have sex; I am definitely far from that, but I get lost in the fear of my cravings and the helpless feelings I have when my desire overtakes me. The idea of losing myself to the clutches of lust and sexual desires scares me. It is the fear that what I hate the most can someday be my downfall. For me, purity and my person go together or should go together; I believed if I lose my virginity, I lose myself. I will lose myself to someone else, and not knowing if that person is ready to take all of me—my dreams, my laughter, my tears—leaves me uncertain about whether having sex is a good idea. To give myself to someone who I am not married to is a great injustice to that person. He will have to love me, keep me, and never leave me and that is too much to ask just anyone. It is enough to ask of true love. It is exactly what true love is when it says, "Take all of me. Take all of me."

This is the belief of my heart, but it is a belief that I have let become tattered and soiled. Temptation is like a whirlwind and *it fills up the world when you are not taking shelter from it. Like so many others, I got tired of holding back, so I began to give myself away in bits and in pieces. First, it was just staying a little longer than I should; then it was allowing the touches that danced like fire across my skin. For that moment, when caresses flowed across my skin and I lost myself in the breath and body of a man, I felt so alive. How could this be wrong? Surely the man felt his heart and soul move in him like a great force, like a wonderful possibility of love and faithfulness when he touched me. Apparently, this was not the case. Finally, I got lost in the hands of an undeserving man who wanted to take it all away. Although I won the battle over my virginity, I lost the fight over my virtue, integrity, and purity.*

I dove into other sexual habits that I felt were without consequence. All of my belief system failed me and I was, once again, looking for love in places where there was no love. My virtue shriveled up and died slowly and painfully as I began to define what virginity really was and how that defined me. It was about who or what I really was and how all my life—at least my dating life—had revolved around the hymen tissue and its validity.

Handicapped by the same standard I had set for myself, I set out to rebel against my own standards. It was like fighting against oneself, beating the air and losing. The very thing I was proud of being began to irritate me. How could this thin veil of flesh be so important? I tried hard to get rid of it, pushing the limits of my own morality, but, when the time came to cross into the unknown, I could not bring myself to lose it. Before I had thought that what was between my legs was what made me a virgin, but I now realized that it was so much more than any tissue or bleeding. It is a state of mind.

Most young women cannot remember exactly when they began their journey to womanhood, but the transition from adolescence to womanhood is often muddled in a smooth procession of events and activities that make it difficult to visibly distinguish the chances of survival. My sexual transition was not so smooth. I did things because I wanted to experiment. I did things because of the messages on television and in magazines that had power over me. The allure of the images and the way they inspired me to look at myself were powerful.

It was not simply about being well-groomed; it was about being devastating to a man's senses. It was about centering my focus on the one aspect of myself that I knew was powerful to not just me but to a man. Although I saw my virginity as some type of trophy that I should present to my husband when I got married, I never thought about what it really meant. I had to deal with my inability to contain my lustful desires. There were things I did and I could not understand why I did them. There were things I watched on television that I could not understand. Memories of two naked bodies having sex right on my television would haunt me for days, maybe even weeks. I walked away from hard-earned principles and dabbled in things that were not pure and, somehow, I yearned for more. Nothing satisfied me.

I have to admit that the pressure is intense to define myself by exhibiting my sexuality through my clothing, my make-up, *and my movements. It feels good to turn heads; it feels good to have men appreciate me and desire me; and it feels good to look in the mirror and see that I can compete with other women for attention. The ways men make me feel are gratifying when they flirt and pursue me with gifts and attentions. I feel strong and powerful for a moment when the man I am attracted to is caught up in my youth and beauty. For a moment, I believe that, maybe, he might love me. It is a frail dream, built on my most fleeting quality, yet I want to believe it will last forever. This is not of God and I know it.*

I put the essay down and sighed. In the morning, I would share it with my friend who was in so much pain that is the result of sin, pain, and regret. As a girl brought up in a Christian home, my morals were set by the standards my parents taught and lived. But, by the age of 18, all my ideals about purity, sex, and virginity had been altered by my peers and through the media. Like so many others, I began to reconstruct my idea of what the creation of my mortal body was about in order to deal with the guilt I felt for not living by the standards I knew to be the best for me. It has been a painful experience to heal from the past. As a married woman I decided to alter the memories of my past and keep them firmly held in God's hand.

Writing this book is the most difficult thing I have ever done—from staying up late and crying through some chapters to praying for forgiveness for all the things I have done in the past and having flashbacks of those things I had, somehow, blocked out of my mind. As a teenager, you never stop to think about how all your actions will affect you later in life. I regret every moment that I let my body take control over my mind and the periods when lustful desires collided with my developing mind.

This compilation is intended to share God's thoughts through my voice. My intention is to get a better understanding of why God created my body and what my purity represents. I understand that maturity in life is a wonderful gift, but if my experiences as a younger woman can help another avoid the pitfalls I have experienced, then I am happy to share even though I am not proud of my youthful indiscretions. Like everyone else, my experiences range from the positive to the negative. However, while writing this book, I have come to realize that because of works such as this, young people can see and better understand themselves. Through works like this book, maybe someone will be spared the sorrow of a life that is not wholly pressed into God's hands.

I did not write this to establish myself as a psychologist or as an expert on human sexuality. I wrote this book because I was once a teenager who knew the types of desires that young people deal with every single day. I also was once a young adult with the same struggles and desires, which grew with time. I am now a married mother who prays desperately for the purity of my sons and believing that I can instill in them the importance of waiting and the beauty of true love.

Knowing now the true meaning of love, knowing that

having sex with anyone you are not married to, depletes the wonderment of YOU. I understand the moments of guilt, pain, regret, low self-esteem, desire, fiery love, and heartbreak, you feel after falling into the arms of an underserving man. I have been torn between two extremes: chastity and lust. After all the ravages of living—from the good to bad and to my wavering spiritual convictions—I somehow managed to emerge as a decent human being. I am now stronger, wiser, and more respectful of the destiny that God has given me.

As a freshman in college, I was unsure of who I was inside. Therefore, I embraced the ideas of my peers and, in turn, forgot some of my own principles. Though professing to be a virgin, I gave in to numerous temptations that confused my dates. Somehow, all those church lessons about chastity and waiting for the right time vanished into thin air when I was held in a tender embrace. I realized the kind of journey I had gone through and how I might be able to use my experiences to help others. I have no qualifications to write about sex and why one should wait for the right time, but, then again, who does have that knowledge? Therefore, I offer my own thoughts and experiences in the world of premarital sex that will cause you to either deride my wrongdoings or recognize and learn from some of the same lessons.

The idea of sex may seem enjoyable and inviting, but it leaves one with pain, hurt, and shame when acted upon at the wrong time in a person's life. Soon, the warm fuzzy feelings are replaced with hatred, heartache, child support checks, or sadly, AIDS and STD's. All that remains are traces of wounds that never go away.

The problem is that we often mistake lust for love. Lust is deceitful and fleeting. Love is patient and enduring. There is no real comparison between the two. Even though there seems to be a common denominator between the physical act of sex and the emotional result, there is a vast difference. Lust costs you in the end while love adds something beautiful to your life that endures not for hours, days or weeks but for years and all of your life. Why would you choose to have less of something wonderful when there is something magnificent waiting for you in God's hands?

I hope that, by reading this book, you will see the vision of becoming the person that God intended you to become. I hope you will break free from the shackles of your soul and freely run the race toward fulfilling your destiny. I hope you come away changed forever. I hope your tears are washed away. I hope you can read this book and realize that everybody makes mistakes, but God can still heal your pain and that there is nothing wrong with waiting until your wedding day. I hope you can laugh, cry, and believe in your own identity in the same way I believe in mine and that you set your ideals and stand on your principles. I hope you find the true meaning of the love of God, and His reason for creating your body. I hope you, the reader, can understand that you are never alone in the struggle between carnal desires and Godly choices. Most of all, I hope you catch a glimpse of the love of God because, in order to come away changed, you need both His love and self-love. So, love yourself the best you can and do not let anyone despise your youth or demean your purity because your body is God's temple.

#What My Mom Taught Me About Sex

Sex education for many starts at an early age. Some learn about the birds and the bees from their parents and others unfortunately at the hands of someone older, robbing them of their innocence and leaving them with painful memories and scars. Still others learn about sex education from a nervous teacher who would rather not teach the subject, the question is who taught you about sex? Those lessons can either make or break your attitudes towards sex. I learned about sex as a teenager. The conversation that started my journey towards womanhood began the first day my mom told me not to have sex.

I had just come home from school and my mother was waiting for me by the door. She asked me to walk with her to the drug store. I was fourteen and the oldest of six, so the idea of actually getting to spend some time alone with my mother and be free from some of my afternoon chores was a pleasant surprise. It was a beautiful, hot day and I set out with my mother with my young girl's heart alight with a moment of freedom and the honor of undivided attention from my mother. After a moment or two of walking together, I noticed my mother was silent as if she was gathering her thoughts. I was curious and, to be honest, a little concerned that, perhaps, I was in trouble for something.

I waited, walking quietly with my mother. She began slowly, speaking to me from her deep places though she struggled to frame her thoughts. She said, "Vivian, you are my oldest and you have four younger sisters. So much of my honor is bound to your honor, and I have to teach you things that you need to know. I have to tell you about the ways of men and how the world works. The world is a hard place for women and harder still if you are the mother of many daughters. That is why I need for you to be a good example to your sisters. It will help me to teach them if I can use you as a good example."

I listened and watched my mother's face. I could see how hard it was for her to talk to me, but I did not know why.

I told her, "If I need to do my chores better, I can do that. I can cook more if that will help."

She replied, "No, no. That is not what I mean. I am talking about boys and men and you keeping yourself a virgin until marriage and keeping the honor of our family intact. I am talking about sleeping with boys."

I said, "Okay. Should I make more room for Prince?" Prince was my little brother and the only son in our family. He usually slept in the men's quarters, but I thought that I could watch him in our rooms at night. Maybe we were going to have a bunch of my male relatives come to stay. I was confused.

She replied, "I am talking about having fun."

My eyes must have grown as big as the moon. In our culture, having fun meant having sex. I was stunned.

"Mommy, I don't have fun!" I sputtered. "I don't do that!"

She said, "Do you have, well, a boyfriend?"

I told her, "No! Even if I did, I wouldn't do that!" I was horrified and, even worse; my mother was so uncomfortable that she was blushing.

She then said, "Well, I still have a duty to teach you about birth control. You must never get pregnant, and touching boys can get you pregnant. You can't even touch one, not one little bit. Don't hold their hands. Don't hug them. Don't let them touch your body at all, not one little touch. You could get pregnant, and then you will have no end of trouble and all your sisters will follow your example."

I asked, "Not even a single touch?"

I looked askance at the men and boys strolling down the street who were going about their business. They looked ominous and frightening. I shuddered at the thought of catching their contagious sperm and getting pregnant.

She answered, "Not even a single touch. It will ruin your life."

I knew for a fact that it was the end of innocence for me. In fact, I was so terrified that I resolved in my heart and soul that I would not even stand close to a man. My honor and future were at stake. My life and the prestige of my family were at stake. It was important for me to avoid the calamity of pregnancy at all costs. For the longest time, if a man came within touching distance, I scurried away from him and his contagious sperm.

Three years after that conversation, I found myself contemplating doing what my mom told me not to do. I got my first kiss and, somehow, I wanted more. In my head, I could hear my mom saying, "Touch a guy and you will get pregnant." Her voice rang through my head every time I made out with a guy. I would hear voices in my head, one belonging to my mom and the other was the voice of my pastor saying, "Have sex and go to hell!" I knew I was in big trouble when, after making out, I would "freak out," thinking something had flown into me and I would get pregnant. Needless to say, I probably scared my dates silly. I basically learned that sex was supposedly wrong for girls. Most of what I learned about sex was the fear of something bad. I believed that I was either going to get pregnant or "go to hell." The fear instilled inside of me had scared me away from making mistakes, but it also made me curious about the sexual act itself.

Undoubtedly, my fears followed me through my early adult years, but I had gotten a little complacent in my approach to waiting to have sex. At 19, I started breaking all the rules. I started dating a guy I knew I would never marry and compromised my beliefs just to please him, which led to a lot of stupid choices and mistakes. I guess my decision to stay chaste was based on the fear instilled in me by the Church and my parents. So, instead of following through with my stand on chastity, I sinned all the time.

At that time, I still had not made a conscious decision to stay chaste. I based my idea of chastity on what others told me instead of on what I knew was the right thing to do. I based my choices on the powerful urges I felt rather than on the gift of reason that is given each of us.

What my mother did not tell me was that sex was an awesome thing; that my virginity was precious and worth more than ten thousand rubies; and that any man who cannot wait for me does not deserve me. My mom told me everything she understood except that the older I got, the more my sex drive would grow and it would be more difficult to stay chaste. She also forgot to tell me how some guys leave when they do not get what they want. Mom also failed to mention that there is more to sex than intercourse. She just told me, "Don't get pregnant," which was what I avoided. We all learn lessons as we grow and those lessons shape our existence, our beliefs and attitudes. You have the choice to make.

#How My Culture Defined Me

I had worked hard my entire life to save myself for marriage. All the while, I had a sex life whether I knew it or not. My concept of virginity has been put to test and I had learned a certain truth, which redefined it. My life and my mind were at the mercy of my virginity. For a long time, I believed in my wholesomeness. To me, losing my virginity was like having Bubba, the ugliest boy in 8th grade, kiss me with his mouth filled with braces, brown teeth, fourth-degree stank breath, and his saliva swimming in my mouth in front of everyone at the school dance. It was a reprehensible idea to be avoided at all costs.

In my culture, a woman who lost her virginity before she married was pretty much doomed. She was dishonored; her family was disgraced; and it was likely that no one would be willing to marry her. She was labeled a whore or loose "Ashewo" (pronounced: *Ah-shea-woe*, the Yoruba word for prostitute). In order for her to find a mate, she would have to change her name, join the choir, act saved, move to another city (preferably a bigger one), and act like a virgin. A woman, who lost it, gave it up, or had it taken by some fool was labeled the same way.

Although I would not be tied to a stake and burnt to death if I lost my virtue, I felt a certain push to keep it no matter what. All my life, I was told to guard my virginity. I was told it was a gift to present to my husband on my wedding night. Although my ambitions were quite admirable and I largely forgotten because of modern encroachment, they still, like the Niger River, course through the veins of the young women and men of my region, and flow like flash floods in the midst of a monsoon as we approach the cycles of love and romance in present times.

I love my tradition and my history. Somehow, I wish the traditions stayed. I want my parents to receive yams and red oil. I want my white bedspread to be stained with blood. I want to be held in honorable stature within my village as well as bask in the affirmation of my loving husband and be exalted as an innocent queen. Like the lioness basks in the Serengeti sun, eyes low and tight at its powerful rays and her head held high in glory of her pride, I also dream of basking in the upholding of my country's honor and glory to bring prestige and approval to all my well-wishers and to my loving West African parents. I come from a country where women were taught at an early age that sex was bad while men were taught the art of conquest. Sex was a subject never discussed in churches, at home, or in schools. But somehow, young females would turn out pregnant at an alarming rate, and suppress the shame by aborting the fetus.

It makes you wonder how a society, suppressed by an idealism, can send young people to hell on earth, leave the married ones unhappy, and can heal this wound. How can we get past this barrier of silence? Ignorance is bliss, but education is freedom. At the tender age of 17, I came to the United States to go to school. I was pulled from the life I knew in Nigeria and transported to a land where sex education is a mandated health class and sex is the cornerstone of the capitalist market. Shocked by this new state of affairs, I was surprised to see my younger peers discussing sex so freely in hallways, at bus stops, and on cell phones in the shopping mall.

"There was knowledge about sex," I thought. But I was wrong; sometimes, even education can keep you bound to ignorance. I began to wonder about my country, Nigeria. My eyes began to be open to the ignorant beliefs about sex that are prevalent in my home country. How can you enjoy a blissful sex life when you get married if you have been taught that sex was bad? How can you eventually enjoy sex if you have been told it is a slimy act reserved for whores outside of wedlock and for proper girls within the sacred walls of the marital hut?

I grew up in a country where sex was never really openly discussed though it was a topic you thought about while lying in bed alone late at night. It was a topic you could not discuss with your parents, and your peers would regard you as a slut if you brought it up. The looks on their faces send you the same message: "Sex is bad, don't do it; don't think about it; and don't ask me." You walked around playing the role of the self-righteous saint and living in hypocrisy. Several things would come to mind but none could be answered because the very thing your parents and society warn you against is the very thing you want to do. I can see it on the faces of my peers; they also want the same thing I want.

Nevertheless, in the land of the free you can think, become, and say whatever you want about sex. In America, you are free to learn about sex, think about sex, and talk about sex. This is a land flowing with milk and honey. I was a scavenger ready to learn because the faces I now saw were faces of curious and well-experienced teenagers.

After four months of living in Florida, I learned about oral sex; after a year, I heard about anal sex. Then, I learned what I embraced years earlier on my bed in Northern

Nigeria like that the night embracing a storm was called masturbation. Although I was innocent of these things before I came to this country. My first boyfriend and I were so innocent that we never even held hands while we were together.

Although my approach and attitude toward sex were conservative, I enjoyed the idea of having someone and holding someone. Even so, I was curious and my body craved touches. I wanted to have sex. I thought about it sometimes and I was not ashamed to admit it. I based my whole life on what my society said was the ideal. I foolishly walked into a cliché life where escaping was not possible. The differences between my own native culture, the American culture, and God's prescribed way of living were tearing me apart.

In Nigeria, after my wedding night, it would be my duty to announce to the world that I was a virgin and how much blood stained the white sheet presented to me by my parents. After passing the virginity test, I would have white stars pasted on my forehead and a certificate confirming my virginity to frame for my children to see. I was to become this trophy wife whose husband regarded me as a holy altar.

I would become a lady that never made noise in bed; that did not move too much or have her own desires; and a lady that just lied in bed and enjoyed the ride. So, all my life, I was supposed to guard my hymen from being torn by sex or otherwise so that I would be entitled to be that woman. All my life, I wanted to be the innocent trophy wife. There was nothing wrong with my ambition. I pursued it because of what my culture dictates, and what my parents advised me. Their expectations compelled me to make them proud. As a teenager, all I could think about was my father marrying my mother as a virgin. My aunt was a virgin when she married and some of my friends were also virgins. So, why should I not be like them and why would I not wait? Every day, I strived to be "Miss Perfect," but the more I tried, the more I failed.

I lived in condemnation for a very long time because I indulged in sexual sins. I wondered why it was difficult for me to control my lustful desires. Why could I not be like my other Nigerian friends? Why did I really want to taste the forbidden fruit? The more I tried searching for answers, the more I realized I wanted more. I wanted sex and I wanted it now. Tired of pretending, I engaged in acts I felt gutsy enough to do. I got tired of suppressing my desires and became nonchalant about the standards that I once believed to be central to my life.

By my sophomore year in college, I had dated about three and a half guys. The last one was a "half" because he did not have enough guts to tell me he was dumping me because of my virginity. The thought of being discarded because of being a virgin still leaves a bitter taste in my mouth. I never slept with any of them, but, progressively, my stand on purity became an issue and, to be honest, it was an issue that this African girl was not ready to deal with.

#How Culture Defines You

As the pastor mounted the pulpit with sweat dripping down his face and his handkerchief in hand, he started the service by praying for boldness to preach well and he encouraged the congregation to open up their hearts to listen to what God has to say. "Mmm—my sermon for today is about se-se-sex. If you have sex, you will go to hell. You will be cursed for life. Girls, you will get pregnant. Sex is bad; don't do it; and don't think about it and you will make it to heaven. No hugging, no necking, no kissing, no dating, no nothing. If you do it, I promise you will be a candidate of Hades and God will turn His back on you."

Man, I had to go to the restroom because fear gripped me so hard that my innards squelched and bubbled inside of me. I almost let a good one loose in church because I was so upset; the fear of Hades, fire and brimstone was raining on my head with the Devil poking me with his pitch fork. Was I scared silly?

The poor boy sitting next to me, Benson, was running a hundred degree fever by now. His eyes were as red as crimson. I knew he was feeling guilty because I had heard he slept with Trisha this past week. They did it in the deacon's house who happens to be his father. Trisha's dad was the pastor. Isn't that something? It was all messed up because everybody thought she was all good and stuff, especially the grown-ups who crowned her the best pastor's kid of the year. I heard her crying in the ladies bathroom after service that Sunday. Everyone who knew about her sinful act looked upon her with disdain. I was almost tempted to ask when she was going to start packing to go to hell, but then I felt sorry for her.

Trisha was a good girl and a great friend who made the wrong choices. Nobody was supposed to know, but big-mouth Sandra had told everyone. By the time next Sunday rolled around, the pastor, his wife, and almost every minister had heard about it. Before the benediction was over, almost every parent in church knew about it. Eyes were roaming to see if Trisha's stomach grew any since they last saw her. On the way home, teens got lectured from their parents about what they knew about sex, boyfriends, and if Trisha taught them any bad thing. I heard her parents and some ministers performed an act of exorcism on both her and Benson to rid them of every evil tie. That was after the butt whooping Trisha's mum inflicted on her during the week.

What a shame because St. Calvary Church was never the same ever again. Trisha was sent away to live with an uncle and Benson never looked at another girl again in church. I even heard rumors that his dad had gotten him castrated. Although I think that this was a little bogus and untrue, I believe it must have felt like that for him. Hades or no Hades, I swore never to even kiss a guy. Well, I only did this until the whole Trisha thing died down.

Individuals in authority and religious organizations usually decide how virginity and sex should be defined. Since you cannot see, feel, smell, or touch virginity, the principles for deciding what a virgin is or is not subjective. Some people have felt that virginity is primarily a physical thing. Others have believed that it is psychological or spiritual. Generally, the people who have gotten to make the decisions about how virginity is defined have been people in positions of power over young women's lives. Parents and older relatives, the society, and, especially, religious authorities have always had a lot of clout in terms of deciding what the criteria for virginity is at any given time.

In history, people in power have decided what happens to a woman who is believed to have lost her virginity. Sometimes, their standards have been cruel or even brutal. Even today, there are cultural expectations that are exacting and harsh for young women to prove their purity. In Muslim Turkey and among the Xhosa and Zulu tribes of South Africa, there are mandated rituals called Virginity Testing where young women are routinely gathered and given pelvic examinations to determine if their hymens are still intact. In Asia, the Middle East, and portions of Africa, girls are married at very young ages to insure their chastity. A child just entering puberty can literally be playing the innocent games of the young one week and be married to a grown man the next.

Of course, the most horrifying measure to preserve a woman's chastity is the practice of female genital mutilation (FGM). This practice is so reviled by most of the world that it has been outlawed in most countries and has been condemned by the World Health Organization (WHO). What is missing from these rituals and mutilations are a firm teaching about the central human truth found in the world. I have to wonder why young men are not taught to love in a higher, better way. Why are there not rituals to teach them to honor and respect purity? Why is it just about whether or not the hymen is still intact? Should not all of our teachings about purity revolve around learning to respect and value each other?

If the heart is in the right place, the body will follow. Yes, hormones rage, but our will is larger than any temptations we face. We are created with a sexual nature and we are all given the guidance to navigate the troubled waters that toss us about like bits of flotsam. How I wish I had known then what I know now when poor Trisha and Benson were reviled and punished for their indiscretion. I would embrace them and pray for them. I would help them heal from their guilt and sorrow.

All my life I have only heard about sex twice in church. Ministers cringe and feel embarrassed to talk about sex. Sex is not spoken about in churches and I have seen pastors sweating at the mere mention of talking about sex from the pulpit. This issue is plaguing us as a whole. Teenage girls are getting pregnant; ministers are having babies out of wedlock; and singles are living together before marriage and engaging in sex in various ways before they say, "I do." Most of them think everything besides intercourse is not sex. Clearly, that is not true.

Every passing Sunday, we go to church and never hear a thing about premarital sex, the girl who got raped, the wife who was abused, or the singles in church that are sleeping together. We hear about everything else but the day-to-day issues that plague us. A lot of young people are hurting, crying inside, and hoping that someone would teach them the truth. Some singles are deeply involved in pornography, fornication, cybersex, sexting, and other sexual habits. The church is so closed up in its own world that there is no support system available for single people.

When the church leaders do talk about sex, it is only to say "don't do it", which is not enough. It is so hard to believe someone telling you about the need to remain chaste when they are married and are having a sexual relationship with their spouse. They just say do not have sex and that is all they say. However, for young people not engage in premarital sex, the church must give reasons why, the consequences, and the advantages of waiting, how to say no, how to start over when they fall, and how God still loves them no matter what. The media is investing time into making sure young people lose themselves in the prowess of sex. Television, music, and peer pressure, are having their minds stolen away from the truth. We are giving the job of educating our singles to the media, and the media is teaching them the wrong things to do.

"Lust indulged became habit,
and habit unresisted became necessity."
— St. Augustine

CHAPTER 3
Are You Ready?

Dear Vivian Speaks,
I am so ready to have sex what's the big deal anyway? I plan to protect myself by making sure we use condoms. Moreover we love each other. Why are Christians so hung up on premarital sex?
Stacy

Dear Stacy;
Wow! You are very straightforward about your desires to have sex and there is absolutely nothing wrong with that. The bible celebrates sex within the confines of marriage alone, as seen in the Songs of Solomon. I remembered reading the book as a teenager and asking why intimacy was vividly celebrated. I realized however the intimacy in the Songs of Solomon describes the stages of a relationship, from the wooing to the marriage night. It was a beautiful depiction of how a relationship should blossom. Overtime, I realized that the main phrase in the scripture, "Do not arouse or awaken love until it pleases", refers to the awakening of sexual desires before the time is right, and until you are ready. God, who created all things,

described sex as very good. Christians are not prudes as the media portrays, we just believe in delayed gratification. As you first stated that you are SO ready for sex, my question is 'Are you sure you are ready for sex?' Sex is no big deal in itself, but what are big deals are the physical repercussions of sexual activities and the emotional stress from a loveless encounter. Several individuals just like you in the bible fell into sexual sins because sex is the one natural desire given to everyone by God. Many people believe safe sex is better than no sex and that using condoms is the best way to have your fun and stay protected. Condoms only reduce the risk of HIV by 85% and 15 to 24 year olds have the highest incidence of HIV infection. Unfortunately, condoms do not protect the heart and are not 100% effective against STDs and pregnancy.

#Don't Give It Away

Can I infect your life with the truth? Give me permission to walk all over your heart and try to lead you to the oasis from the desert of lies you have been traveling through. Let me show you a pathway through the desolation of your secrets. Let me help you find a shelter from shame and regret.

Talk to me and do not be afraid. You want to be free, don't you? You want to be triumphant over your own impulses, don't you? You want to be filled with the peace and sweet security of true love, right? You have been around and, although you have not gone all the way, the distance you have gone has made you weary and dissatisfied. You miss your innocence. Now, you want to reclaim your innocence like I reclaimed mine. It is a hard task, so are you ready for the fight? Even if you have had intercourse before, do not fret.

Arise and be free to walk in integrity and honorable chastity. Give yourself the chance to be respected, loved, and cherished. Be happy with yourself, listen to your inner voice, and walk into life with your head held high. You will rejoice in times to come; your wounds will be mended; and your heart will be repaired. You do not need a doctor for this surgery; all you need is to stand and tell yourself: "I am starting over. I am ready to wait. I love myself. And I am ready to take this journey with God on my side." The layers will begin to fall off and the wounds will begin to close up. The healing process is the most painful. While it is not easy, but I believe it is possible. Go on and do not be afraid. Yeah, that's it. Break through to the end.

Sex?

"When a woman has lost her chastity, she will shrink from no crime."
[Lat., Neque femina amissa pudicitia alia abneurit.]
— Tacitus (Caius Cornelius Tacitus), Annales (IV, 3)

CHAPTER 4:

Sex, Sex, Sex:
Going Out To Making Out, Hooking Up To Breaking Up.

Sex! Sex! Sex! I am so excited you made it to this page without pulling your hair out. This section is surprisingly the most important part of the book. I believe if we all know why sex is so important, then we would be in a better place to make good decisions about how we give ourselves away. At 16, all you know of sex is the illusion of endless fun and expression of love that probably does not exist. The number one thing I would love for you to take away after you close these pages and forget about this book and the author is that: SEX IS BEAUTIFUL, and possibly the best thing God created for humans to enjoy.

The purpose of my writing this book is not to drill in your head what to do or not to do. I believe you know right from wrong and can make reasonable decisions about your body. This book is designed to give you the important information about the pros and cons of sex and to help you learn from my mistakes and make your own decisions. Sex is beautiful and a wonderful experience better left for marriage.

There are a lot of people who feel like abstinence is not a good idea and young people should be given the freedom to choose. I believe abstinence is not the key word and should not be hammered into your head. I believe in giving humans choices, even God gave us a choice (choose life that you might live), so with that in mind, in this section we will explore the different types of sexual activities there are, the myths about sex, the truth about sex, the consequences of sex when acted upon at the wrong time and finally the beauty of sex and why it should be savored, and saved for the right person.

The beauty of my new life as a married woman reveals the sacred aspect of sex, and its beauty. I am now amazingly free to express that side of me without holding back. However, with every breath I wish I had saved myself completely for my spouse. The feeling of indescribable peace that is felt when your body is given to the right person at the right time is one that cannot be overstated and is at its best, the most wonderful way to say I love you. I believe saving that aspect of your life keeps it untainted by thoughts of past encounters.

Sex is an amazing expression of the true heart of a human and an intended act to assist God in the process of procreation. Sex is a gift from God, nothing to be ashamed of. Sex opens you up to several emotions, and leaves you vulnerable and unguarded. Sex will keep two people joined together even when they are apart and creates a covenant relationship that is not easily broken.

Logically, you may say well, "I am not having sex," and rightly so, but are you making out, kissing, masturbating, etc. Recently a single friend of mine went out with a guy she met in school and after three dates they started making out, and eventually hooking up at his apartment. The day after what she considered the best sex of her life, she never heard back from him. He never called her and even after numerous attempts she was forced to count her losses and move on. She now hides her face in shame when they run into each other at events or on campus. I have also known men who broke up with ladies after sleeping with them, just to move on to the next best thing. I am not by any means saying sex tears relationships apart, but sex with the wrong person ends badly almost always.

#If We Can't Have Sex, How Far Can We Go?

A frequent question single people ask me is, "How far can we go?" There isn't a ground rule on what not to do and what to do before marriage. Many young people use this to mean that foreplay is fair game as long as they don't have sex. Foreplay, petting, and all are acts to prepare you for sex and are gravely discouraged before marriage. I highly recommend you do not go past holding of hands or hugging while dating, to protect you from falling into temptation.

Any form of kissing before marriage can and will lead to other forms of foreplay and should be avoided at all cost.

#What If It Is Already Too Late?

What if you have already engaged in premarital sex? When I gave myself away at the age of 27 for the first time, I believed my life was over, simply because, for so long I had held on to my virginity and guarded it jealously. But one night of carelessness in the arms of a man I thought I couldn't live without drove me into eating the forbidden fruit. However, after a year of self-pity, and regret, I decided to forgive myself and move on. You can gain a renewed sense of purity and truly rededicate your sexuality to God and make a commitment to Him to remain sexually pure until marriage. Get an accountability partner to help you, tell them about your new commitment and make sure they are grounded enough to help you through your journey. Regain your purity and be determined to save yourself for your spouse. Do not let regret keep you down. God can forgive the sin of premarital sex. He forgave me.

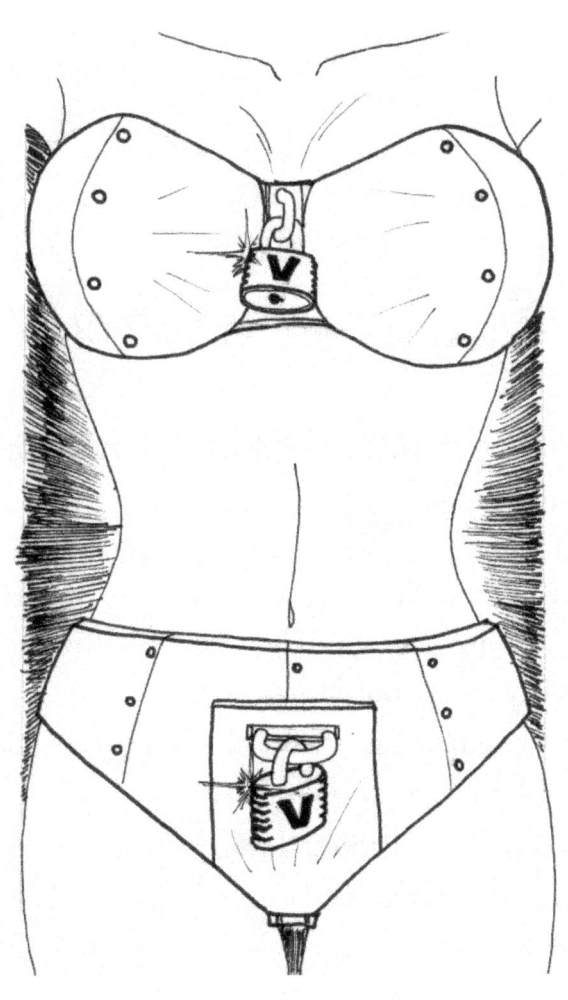

"A daughter is a mother's gender partner, her closest ally in the family confederacy, an extension of herself. And mothers are their daughters' role model, their biological and emotional road map, the arbiter of all their relationships."
— Victoria Secunda

CHAPTER 5
Sex, Virginity, What?

#Defining What Virginity Really Is

I decided that I needed to take stock of my sexual activities. Funny enough, as a so-called virgin, I had a sex life and an active one at that. My dates were probably very confused but played along with me. The rules were these:

1. Avoid getting "popped."
2. Replace intercourse with anything else and do not classify those activities as sex.
3. Do not feel bad about doing the alternatives.

The problem was that every time I persuaded myself not to feel guilty about having a sex life, I would feel even worse. I was becoming a tease who gave up some of myself to men that I had no plans of spending the rest of my life with.

As I pondered my dilemma, I could not find an easy answer. I found solace in the fact that, for once in my life, I was trying to do the right thing. I wanted to truly be a virgin in its entirety and give myself up to self-discipline and self-control. I did not have the squeaky clean record most people look for, but the beauty about life is that you can always change your direction and make it for the better. A year before I got married I decided to re-evaluate my dating life and my choices. The serious self-reflection has been a painful, yet, beautiful journey and an evolution of my spirit and soul. What I realized was that I had built this self-centered view—a box to keep me focused on my goals of waiting and a wall to keep the wolves out. But the walls were built by me and not by God. On my own, there is no possible way to remain pure. It takes support, spiritual confidence, humility, and prayer. I realize that the box I built was faulty; it was not very strong and the walls had cracks in them. All the while, my box has been shifting and giving me room to make some stupid choices and the cracks on the walls provided opportunity to needy men who wanted my body.

Inevitably, I fell into a spiral of unending dangerous behavior that left me disoriented and confused. The same box I had set for myself became my greatest enemy and my hindrance. I needed to be freed from the demands of my prison.

Like other singles in America, I have been one of those that avoided intercourse at all cost but fell into diverse temptations. Out of my own free will, I have crossed boundaries and tip-toed around evil. I have given into lust and fought hard-earned morals. To be honest with you, most of the decisions and choices made when it came to sex were not my date's fault; it was mine because I wanted what I experienced just as much as he did. I would justify my wrong doings by redefining the act and considering it to be morally superior to intercourse. I would console myself and tame my guilt by thinking that my actions held no emotional consequences.

However, just like intercourse, the same consequences apply. Emotional hurt, heart break, low self-esteem, and rejection are all components of ending any relationship, and the sorrow is amplified by the guilt of having given away what is not mine to give until the time is right. Even worse, there are physical consequences that can also apply by contracting diseases like herpes, HPV, syphilis, genital warts, and, even worse, AIDS. There is no high or lower class of goodness or evil. Good is good and evil is evil. Sex is sex no matter what people say.

#When Curiosity Kills The Virgin

Jackie would have walked away from her annoying friend Lisa as she told her tales of every sexual encounter she had. She gloated as she recounted stories of when, where, and how she did it. Jackie, who was inexperienced at the time, chuckled and was disgusted as the stories got nastier. "It is not that bad," Lisa insisted. "Just try it once," Lisa said while walking towards her car.

That night, Jackie felt it was time to go further with John, her boyfriend of three months. After the movies, as John drove her home, she decided to perform oral sex. Shocked at first, John went along with the plan. "Thanks babe," John said buckling his belt. A month later, Jackie developed a nasty wart on her upper lips. Apparently, John had contracted herpes from one of the girls he slept with and now Jackie had it too.

Her first sexual experience was probably based on curiosity. She heard about or saw a sexual activity and became curious and wanted to know how it felt and how far she could go without getting caught. When you engage in sexual activities because you are curious, you are setting up a pit for yourself and you may end up hurt. When ladies participate in sexual activities, it is usually out of curiosity and, sometimes, peer pressure. It is important to make up your mind long before someone comes along to tempt you. When your mind is made up, you have the ability to ignore those feelings and the nagging desire to have sex.

Curiosity would make you want to have sex, watch pornography, and date the wrong men. Deciding to hold out on sexual activity is a very admirable thing to do. For some holding out means not having intercourse and indulging in other sexual activities instead. Unfortunately, when it comes to sexual activities, all of them carry the same emotional and spiritual consequences. It is very important to know the reasons why you are holding out. For me, I was holding out for spiritual reasons, which is the most important reason that can keep a person from heartache and physical consequences.

The decision to hold out is not something you can do on your own. It is important to involve others, such as your close friends, your parents, your spiritual counselor, or the person you are going out with. You cannot hold out if you indulge in other sexual activity because eventually you will give in. A lot of so-called virgins will tell you that they are waiting until marriage for sex, but they indulge in other risky sexual behaviors. These sexual activities carry the same consequences. You lose your soul in the process and lose your respect. Your relationship with God can be severed, leaving you empty and lonelier than before. Emotional attachment is another effect of any sexual encounter. You become emotionally connected to this person that may eventually break your heart. Save yourself the trouble and wait because it is more peaceful and honorable.

#When Your Body Cries

We have been designed to have sex, reproduce, and multiply. Our body goes through hormonal changes that affect how we react to sexual stimuli. There are certain times of the month that are more difficult than others. You may be turned on when you see sexually charged movies, but, other times, it does not affect you.

Some women experience more of this during their ovulation period. You feel like you need to have sex or get close to someone. It is okay for your body to cry for a touch, but, in moments like this, you can tame your body. One of the ways to do this is to avoid movies, music or books that encourage you to let your passions run wild. The question is not if, but rather, when your body cries.

Managing yourself is a challenge during these times, so do not lose yourself to the clutches of lust. Give in to self-control and understand that sex is a natural and universal truth of human existence designed by God to be explored between a man and a woman in holy matrimony.

"The sweetness of sin, the guilt of eating the forbidden fruit, that leaves a taste of satisfaction on the tip of your tongue—the fear of touching heaven but, yet fearing hell."
— Vivian Speaks

CHAPTER 6
Sex, E.T.C.

#What Is Sex? Really!

Here it is: the plain and simple truth. Sex is not just intercourse; it is also physical intimacy that stimulates you with the purpose of one or both persons participating in the act of achieving an orgasm. Sexual behaviors can include masturbation, and we will discuss that in this chapter as well as other sexual acts. So, hold on to your hat, let's get personal, and speak the truth in as honest a manner as we can.

#Fondling

On an episode of *Seinfeld,* Elaine speculates with Jerry about when sex happens. Jerry says that he considers that a person is having sex as soon as the nipple gets involved and that is a good place to start with this discussion. When do we know that we are beginning to cross the line? When you begin to touch anything that is covered by undergarments, you are becoming too sexual. Anything that is normally covered by a bra and panties is a hands-off zone. Anything that is covered by a man's underwear is a no-touch zone. Even through clothing, a heavy coat, a space suit, or a suit of armor, these are places that are reserved for the marriage bed. If a complete stranger were to come up to you and touch your breast, he could be arrested and charged with a crime. If the law takes touching these areas as being private, so should a young person.

Now, what is the big deal? The more you experience outside of the profound depth of true love ends up diminishing the experience of true love. It steals the wonder of some of the most precious moments of your life. Giving away bits and pieces of yourself cheapens the sensations of the first time. In your innocence, the honorable man that God has given you touches you for the first time. Having experience in bed does not necessarily mean that you will be a great lover and it does not mean that you will have a magnificent orgasmic experience.

Experience in bed, outside of love and commitment, only means you have used up some of your potential wonder with the wrong man. Letting someone touch you, even through your clothes, is selling yourself short; it is selling your future short; and it certainly sells your partner short. He deserves to feel a sense of wonder and fulfillment too. Keep your hands to yourself and insist that he keeps his hands to himself as well. If he dumps you, then he is not the man you wanted to experience intimacy with anyway.

#Masturbation

Okay, here it is, the big "M" that we all struggle with. I have to admit that this is the one that is hard to define and hard to deal with because, really, it is the hardest to resist. After all, who gets hurt? Who else has been involved with you? How can you help it if you intend to remain pure? Sometimes, celibacy can make you want to scream and tear your hair out and it seems like masturbation is the only answer. Frankly, maybe, sometimes, it is the only way to manage a very strong sex drive. The bible teaches that a man that has had a nocturnal emission, or a wet dream, is considered unclean and has to be ritually purified, but it is unclear if masturbation is strictly forbidden.

The difficulty about masturbation lies, not so much in the physical act, but more in the fantasies that accompany the act. Let's face it; what happens in real life is not exactly what happens in our fantasies. No doubt, there was some time in history when a princess was rescued from some terrible villain and no doubt she was thankful. She may have even fallen in love with her rescuer and lived happily ever after. No doubt this was happily ever after once she became accustomed to his smelly feet and his obsession with swords. Reality comes with warts and a certain amount of odor that is unavoidable. In our fantasy world, our lover seduces us with an expertise that is astounding and we are left a trembling heap of satisfied desire. In real life, our hair gets accidentally tangled in a watch band; our clothes get terribly wrinkled; and all the wrestling and rolling about might just make us want to burp in an unladylike fashion. These things never happen in our fantasy life. In our fantasy life, we are always perfect and so is the object of our desire.

Our friends and peers might be telling us that everything is perfect when they have sex, but if you have an experienced adult woman to confide in, chances are she will tell you that, even with a very exceptional sex life, it is not what the media portrays. Personally, for them, it is better, but it is real and comes with responsibility and some mess. I know that my fantasy experience will not be as earthy and sweaty as my true life experience will be and I can accept that. It is about expectations and the belief that God has what is best for you in His perfect plan. We are physical beings and, perhaps, masturbation is the escape valve we need to survive being single. I just cannot say for sure. If you are obsessed with your own pleasure, then you need to spend some time on your knees in holy prayer. I am not suggesting that you all go home and masturbate, but I am saying that you have to constantly lift every aspect of your life up to the Lord and examine yourself carefully in the light of God's perfect love. Avoid lying with pillows between your thighs, limit the time your spend lying in the bath tub, avoid sexual movies, and, most importantly, pray.

#Oral Sex

For many years, there was very little said out loud about oral sex. When I was younger, I had never heard of oral sex and, to be honest, the notion never crossed my mind. I did not think it was possible. My first reaction when I heard about oral sex was to screw my face up and say, "Eeeuuwwwww!" I could not imagine anyone wanting to do that. To be honest, I think that some cultures are more accepting of oral sex and find it just a part of natural lovemaking. Notice that I put it into the category of lovemaking. That means sex. Hmmmmm.

If there is an erection involved; if there is an orgasm involved; and if there is direct contact with any part of the body that is typically covered by underwear, you are having a sexual experience. Again, there are no specific passages in the scriptures that regulate oral sex, but anyone that is honest and has experienced oral sex cannot say they have not had sex.

#Anal Sex

Anal sex is probably the most damaging sex act that exists. Let's face it, inserting anything in a thrusting manner into a part of the body that is designed to expel only is going to eventually hurt a person's body. The walls of the anus are absorbent and the muscles are easily damaged. God destroyed Sodom and Gomorrah to show his disapproval for this particular sex act. He designed our bodies in a particular manner and He intends for us to use our bodies as they are designed.

Many who are on the receiving end of anal sex are hurt by the experience and can suffer from the discomfort for days afterward. The irritated body can develop hemorrhoids, intestinal infections, and an interruption of the natural cleansing process that is so very important to maintain a healthy body. I am not an expert on this subject and

I understand there are members of society that live an alternative lifestyle that will strongly disagree with me, but I have to caution my readers about this damaging sexual expression. If your boyfriend wants to have anal sex, then just look him in the eyes and tell him "no."

#Mutual Masturbation

This is another sex act that, although it can be convenient and can relieve pent up sexual energy without disturbing the hymen, it is still sex. Remember that fondling through clothing is sex and rearranging clothing in order to touch the body directly is certainly sex. If it should be covered up and untouched in church, then it must be covered up and untouched everywhere you are until you are married. Of course, after marriage, all bets are off and you can be naked if you mutually want to be naked together. You still need to behave properly in public, but, in the privacy of your home, enjoy each other.

#Cybersex/Phone Sex/Sexting

Be honest, the sole purpose of this pastime is to inspire the person on the other end of the message board or telephone line to respond sexually. It is talking to a person that does not love you and is not into you enough to actually be in the same room with you. Again, it is a fantasy and fantasies are not what God has for you. Sexting can affect you later on in life, say you sent a naked picture of yourself to your boyfriend, then a week later you break up, and he sends off your picture to all his friends, and his friends post it online. Hmmmmmm!

#Pornography

Looking at pornography is, again, building a fantasy out of nothing that is real. The people in the videos are actors and they are acting like they are having fabulous sex. People in pornographic pictures are posed and they are acting like they are enjoying a fantastic sexual experience. It is not cool; it is not real; and it is not something that glorifies God. These actors and models are lost in lives that are demeaning and painful. It is not good to neglect the soul of a person just to gratify a need you feel is not worthy of you. As Gods child, you need to feel pity for those who have lost themselves in this industry. If you are posing for pornographic photos, then you have turned yourself into an object and, again, I cannot stress enough that you deserve to be respected, so respect yourself and stop being less than God wants.

This is not an exhaustive list of sexual activities and, truthfully, I do not know much more than I have presented to you. I cannot advise you about fetishes because I do not know anything about them. I cannot tell you about homosexuality because I am not one. What I can tell you about and the advice I can give you is this: God has a plan of forgiveness for each of us and he loves us so much He made the ultimate sacrifice of His only begotten Son so that we might be saved. Embrace your salvation. Glory in it, revel in it, and celebrate it. Search the scriptures for the truth. Let the Holy Spirit guide your steps. Love yourself as God loved you so much so that he gave his life and conquered death for you. See yourself through God's eyes and draw close to our Heavenly Father. A happy result of a close walk with God is purity of thought, word, and deed. It is not impossible and it is worth your best efforts.

#The Myth And The Truth About Sex

SEX MYTH AS TOLD BY THE MEDIA
(What The World, The Media, Magazines, Celebrities, Presidents, And Lady Gaga Probably Told You About Sex)

1. We are told that sex is everything. We are taught to believe that a good day ends in bed entwined in the arms of a lover. Television programs portray the end of every conflict between a man and woman as resolved by a passionate sexual encounter. The message is clear: Sex cures all of the problems and is the reward for every triumph.

2. We are told that sex makes you cool and attractive. Witness the abundance of television, magazine, movies, and cyber attractions that center around sex. Sex sells. Beautiful people are sexy people. The more beautiful you are, the more amazing your sex life is likely to be.

3. Oral sex is not sex. I could quote a famous politician at this point, but we all know what he said about oral sex. Oral sex is just harmless recreation.

4. Sex outside of marriage is okay. Life is short, passion is fleeting, and we have to grab each moment we can to feel fulfilled and complete. Regrets are only in your mind and you need to be freed from them to live life naturally and freely. God loves freedom.

5. Abstinence is impossible. We are creatures that are controlled by our hormones. Human attractions are powerful and can bring great release and meaning to your lives. It is the most natural expression between a man and a woman and should not be prevented. We do not need another frustration.

6. Virginity is archaic. It is unsophisticated to be a virgin. Virginity is just another way to stigmatize women. It is another way for men to control women and keep them repressed. In order to be on equal footing in this man's world, we need to be free to express ourselves sexually as men have throughout history. Virginity is not a big deal.

7. Sex outside and within marriage is the same. If you love someone, sharing your body is the best way to express your love. Marriage is the next step in love. Living together and being intimate frees a couple up to explore other issues about their relationship because they are not distracted by the effort it takes to remain celibate.

8. There is no need to save sex for marriage. You can have sex once you meet someone you love. Besides, don't men have an appreciation for a woman who

knows what she is doing in the bedroom? Experience is a good thing and it only makes you better able to please your partner if you have the knowledge that will make you a good lover.

9. Sex makes you popular and everybody is doing it. It is hard to be left out of the loop when you are talking to your friends. I want to be a part of the big picture and virgins are simply nerds that cannot attract attention. I want to be part of the conversation!

10. Whatever you do aside from intercourse is not really sex. Intercourse is the only way to get pregnant, so it is really the only thing that needs to be avoided. If God wanted us to abstain from other types of sexual pleasure, wouldn't He have made something like a hymen for those parts as well? Let's face it, it is natural and it helps us release our sexual frustrations to have alternatives.

MEDIA MYTH BUSTERS

1. Do not be deceived. Sex is not everything. To focus on one part of your life is denying the glory, the possibilities, and the power of everything else God has for you. So often we are so intent on our sexuality that it narrows our vision. Consider all of nature, the rocks, and the trees. Consider the innocence of children playing and the satisfaction of a relationship with a dear pet. Think about time spent with the elderly and wise ones in your life. None of these

things have anything to do with your sex life. Live a complete life by filling it up with curiosity about the world, service to the needy, affection for the family, and spiritual sharing. Do not limit yourself to just one thing about a relationship. Here is a true thing, listen carefully, and understand this: Men and boys are not just about sex. Men and boys can be better and greater than just the pursuit of a sexual encounter. Try talking to them. Share interests. Love them in a pure way and you will find that they value you more than they ever imagined they could treasure a woman. Believe this: men are better than you think if you give them the chance to be better than you think.

2. Sex does not and will not make you cool or more attractive. Although you may temporarily gain recognition from your peers, that attention can be short lived. If you go to any hospice where victims of AIDS are suffering through their last days, you can clearly see that the result of unsanctified sex is devastating. Go to the special schools for pregnant teenagers and visit with them for a day, help an unwed mother tend to her child, and it will all be very clear that the end result of a sexual relationship is not easy to endure. Dying and sacrificing your youth and future are not sophisticated or cool. Herpes is not cool. Syphilis is not cool. Gonorrhea is not cool. Go to the clinic where they treat sexually-transmitted diseases and see if it is something you want to experience. I would think not. Ask therapists and those in the

mental health industry about how many of their patients suffer from their sexual mistakes and I am certain you will be overwhelmed. Sex outside of a loving marriage is a painful, empty experience and that is not cool.

3. Oral sex is sex. Oral sex is a form of sexual expression. Oral sex carries the same physical, emotional, and spiritual consequences as vaginal intercourse except without the possibility of pregnancy. A good rule of thumb is this: If an erect penis is entering your body anywhere, it is sex. If your boyfriend says it is the only way he can express his feelings for you, then suggest that he gives you flowers instead. He can get a very nice bouquet at Wal-Mart for a reasonable price. Prove your affection for your sweetheart in a sweet way, light touches, laughter, and shared thoughts. This is a truer way to get to know the soul of a man, and, trust me, getting to know the soul of a man is a worthwhile adventure. Believe that they are better and finer than their erections.

4. Sex is great but sex outside of marriage is not okay because it can produce irreparable scars. The binding of two people in the marriage bed is a holy event, blessed by God, and untouched by any shame. It is private but unhidden. It is no one's business and has few consequences that are not expected. When children come to a married couple, it complicates their

lives, but never like the way it complicates the life of an unmarried person. When a couple is monogamous, there is very little likelihood of a sexually-transmitted disease. When the deep love of a committed marriage is in place, the sexual relationship grows and improves. If you ever get a chance to talk frankly with an older married couple about their sex lives, you will be surprised at their contentment. Practice makes perfect and it can take years to truly understand how to please your partner. Fleeting sexual experiences rob you of the opportunity to experience true passion.

5. Abstinence is about self-control and it is possible. Let's face it, abstinence can make you want to pull your hair out by the roots. Sexual energy is intense and compelling, but it can be channeled into other, more productive, endeavors. How many great books, works of art, pieces of music, and altruistic works have been created by those that are celibate? It would be impossible to calculate. Each of those great individuals who have chosen to remain celibate and dedicatee their lives to something greater than themselves were persons with a sex drive that had to learn to put their energy into something greater than themselves.

6. Virginity is actually cool and is not only for the women from the 1800s. Someone who is strong enough to be a virgin knows herself and knows what she wants. Virgins insist that the man she loves gets to know her thoughts and feelings. She insists that someone value

and treasure her. Anyone strong enough to be a virgin in today's world will get what she wants because she has not sold herself short. Even better, she has not sold the man she loves short either. She has believed in his honor and self-control and she has not been wrong.

7. Sex outside of marriage is fake. It is based on lust and it is not pure. On the other hand, sex within marriage is divinely designed to be real, based on love, and it is pure.

8. There is a need to save sex for marriage. Most people who waited to have sex had a higher level of intimacy with their spouse and were much happier with other aspects of their marriage. I have never met anyone that has been sorry they have waited for marriage.

9. Sex does not make you popular and not everybody is doing it. Popularity is not the most important experience in the world. Popularity bought at the expense of your soul is too expensive. You are worthy wherever you stand in the pecking order of your environment. Certainly, popular people seem to be having a good time, but you cannot know whether or not they are truly happy or if they feel the weight of their actions dragging them into sorrow and loneliness. Wouldn't you rather be popular because you have a kind and loving nature? Isn't being a strong, healthy young woman who is living a life of unbounded possibility more attractive than living a momentary, empty existence? Believe in yourself and ignore the

lure of giving yourself away to just gain recognition from a bunch of bone-headed young adults that cannot function in society without compromising themselves. Live deeply and with the strength of your faith to hold you up.

10. Whatever you do sexually aside from a peck on the cheek is really sex. Enough said.

SEXUAL MYTHS AS TOLD BY THE CHURCH
(What Your Clergy, Pastor, Priest, Or Rabbi Probably Told You About Sex Though They Would Rather Not Have Said A Thing)

1. Sex is bad. All sex is bad. It is bad to think about sex. No Christian ever has sex and no Christian will ever have sex. Let us not talk about sex.

2. It is easy to abstain from sex. We should all be so deliriously happy in Christ every second of the day with reading our Bible all day and spending hours in contemplative prayer that there is, of course, no time for thoughts about sex.

3. Once you have sex, then you are doomed to hell. There is no room for this weakness. If you were doing all the things you should be doing, then this would not be an issue.

4. Sex should not be exciting. Although it is necessary for the future of the human race, keep it quick and do not dwell on it.

5. You should not be tempted to have sex. If you are perfect, you will not be thinking about these things. God can make you perfect.

CHURCH MYTH BUSTERS

1. Sex is very good because God created sex for married people to enjoy and reproduce the human race. It is an awesome thing to share with a man you love within marriage.

2. It is not easy to abstain from sex. It is a struggle and a fight because it is natural for a human, especially after a certain age, to crave sex. Abstinence requires self-control and patience which humans have to develop as they grow older.

3. Once you have sex, then you can be separated from God because of the sin of fornication, but you are not doomed to hell once you repent and turn away from sin.

4. Most people have been fed this lie for centuries and have been ensnared by it. Sex, which God created for marriage alone, should be exciting, fun, and an exploration of the one you love. It is an act of worship to God and a form of praise. Having sex is a way of thanksgiving. It is a way of thanking God for creation, your spouse, the beauty of the body, and the power of love. Sex is like music and dancing. If there were no music or dances on earth, then life would be very boring.

5. Everyone gets tempted. It is God's design that we be triumphant over sin, so, as a result, we are going to be tested. Temptation will come your way. In fact, the moment you decide to do the right thing, temptation will raise its ugly head, but that is not sin. Just flee from it and do not fall. Make yourself accountable to a friend, a mentor, or a near relative. Do not go to places where you know you will be tempted. If going to the mall and flirting leads you into doing things that you are ashamed of later, go to the mall with your mother. Even if she does not have the greatest taste in clothing, in 'your opinion, she loves you enough to keep you safe. If reading spicy romance novels leads you astray, read some other type of book. There are many amazing books in the world that can fill your mind with wonder and inspire you to greater heights. Choose well. The scriptures teach us to flee from temptation and resist the Devil so do just that.

SEX MYTHS AS TOLD BY YOUR PARENTS
(What Your Mom, Dad, Nana, Papa Or Guardian Probably Told You About Sex And Felt Guilty About Because They Knew They Were Not Telling You What You Needed To Know. Chances Are They Were Dying Of Embarrassment.)

1. Touch a guy and you will get pregnant. Breathe on a man and they will instantly jump all over you and molest you. Men only have one thing on their mind and to have any peace with them you will have to compromise everything, so avoid them.

2. Sex is very bad. It is disgusting. The only reason animals have sex is because they go into heat and cannot help themselves. If they had a choice, they would never have sex. You have a choice, so never have sex.

3. Women are not to be sexual except for those morally deformed ones. It is all about the men. Men are animals. They are depraved and only have one thing on their minds. Even the good ones are animals.

4. Sex is a shameful act.

5. Sex is dirty.

MOM'S MYTH BUSTERS

1. Touching a guy will not get you pregnant but intercourse will. Most parents say this to girls to save them from having sex. In my culture, girls grow up still thinking that once a guy touches them they will turn up pregnant, They get so scared of sex and end up bringing that fear into the marriage. Even with the more open atmosphere found in this country, sometimes mothers will turn men into monsters in their daughter's eyes. The natural instinct of a mother is to protect her child from danger. So, when it comes to sex and when and if a mother talks to her child, she tells her that sex is bad, particularly if she is not happy with her own sex life or if she has learned lessons about life the hard way.

2. You have to consider the fact that your mother is more experienced than you are and she is trying to do the best she can for you. Remember when you were younger and you went close to a stove while your mom was cooking? Remember how she yelled and told you it was bad? "Hot, hot, it'll burn you," She said. She did not want you to get burned by the stove. You got scared and, for a very long time, you did not go near a stove, but, hopefully, the stove does not scare you anymore. Well, the problem is not the stove itself but the danger the stove poses when it becomes hot. Similarly, it is the same with sex. Your mom probably told you it was bad and if you as much as touch a man you will get pregnant. What your mom did not tell you is that a stove is harmless when it is cold, but when you turn it on, it gets very hot. Men are like stoves. When they are cold, they are safe but when they get hot, you could get burned.

3. Most women grow up with the notion that sex is bad, dirty, and wrong. There cannot be any finger pointing because we only pass down what we have learned over time to other generations. So, a mother who tells her daughter that sex is wrong probably learned that from her mom and it keeps on streaming down and, if it is not broken, then a lie becomes truth if it is well said and believed over time by a number of people. A mother's mechanism to keep you from having sex and getting hurt is to tell you that it is bad. Sex, in

itself, is the most amazing expression of love created by God for two emotionally mature adults in holy matrimony. What your mom failed to tell you is that sex is good and that it is the most intimate of love expressions. It is a divine, deep connection between two people. Once they come together intimately, then their souls become one.

4. You are created as a sexual being by God and women are sexual beings. Your body was designed to please your spouse. The key is expressing this at the right time with the right person.

5. Sex is beautiful and is nothing to be ashamed of. Nothing God created should be demeaned.

6. Sex is not dirty, but most women carry this myth into their marriage bed. They are uncomfortable with their bodies; they feel dirty after having sex; and they feel bad or guilty and some never give themselves the chance to enjoy sex. Sex is clean, good fun for those who are married. It is an intimate moment for married individuals. Break those chains and enjoy sex after marriage.

Do not buy those lies told by the media, parents, churches, and other people. Myths told by parents may be a way to protect you from the unknown. Sex is great and beautiful as well as worth saving for that special someone. If you have had sex before or you are struggling with it now, just be encouraged and you will find the strength to stop.

Listen to people, but filter what you hear and choose what makes more sense to you. The one thing almost all of these people agree on is that sex before marriage is limited. It limits you and can cause problems after marriage. People who waited had a better sex life during marriage and were more likely to be faithful to their spouse. I hope you can bust the myths out there and not fall prey to the lies.

#Sex: Save It!

I hope you have learned quite a few things about sex you possibly didn't know before. I also hope you have decided to take the journey to save sex for marriage; not because I said so, but because you have so much more to offer a man or woman than your body. You have so much more beauty than what is seen outwardly. Living your life with reckless abandonment is something you may end up regretting in the long run. Live your life with no regrets of the past and fear of the future. Sex has its consequences, STDs, heartache, unexpected pregnancies, breakups, and tainted integrity. You have a choice to make; premarital sex is not about sin necessarily, it is about saving your soul from death.

#Okay, Point Taken!
#So Is It Okay To Have Sex?

That is one question I hear all the time when I talk to teens and singles. Maybe your boyfriend/girlfriend or fiancée is pressuring you about having sex and you feel the need to just do it and get it over with or maybe your relationship is progressing in that direction and you are wondering what to do the next time you are nestled up in a tight space in your date's car. Everyone is doing it, so why not you? As a teenager, the only thing that kept me from having sex was the fear of getting pregnant and the degradation of being labeled a whore. In my mind, I weighed the positive and negatives of having sex and decided that waiting was the best option for me. But as soon as I got to college my next question was, what base could I cross?

A lot of young people believe that anything below the belt is off limits, so they cross the line by kissing, cuddling and arousing untimely intimacy. The problem with this is that we don't know when to stop. Eventually, we might get caught up in the moment, lose our heads and hit a home run. What God then created to be a beautiful and poetic expression of pure love is now followed with regret and feelings of guilt, shame, and embarrassment.

In the bible it states plainly, "But among you there must not be even a hint of sexual immorality, or of any kind of impurity, or of greed, because these are improper for God's holy people." From these verses, we see that the Bible promotes complete and total abstinence from premarital sex.

When you save sex for marriage you are saving your own life, protecting yourself from having babies you cannot afford, honoring God with your body and placing value on your body.

Wait!

"As soon as you willfully allow a dialogue with temptation to begin, the soul is robbed of peace, just as consent to impurity destroys grace."
— St. Josemaria Escriva

CHAPTER 7

Waiting Sucks, But The Wedding Night Is Awesome!

Most people would expect their wedding night to be: calm, beautiful and a state of euphoria. The honeymoon night was designed for couples to enjoy unrestricted sex for the first time. The earliest reference to the honeymoon dated as far back as the bible. A man was supposed to take off military duty and work to spend one whole year with his new wife. Honeymoon in the 1800's was assumed to be the wife's sexual initiation period. The first time was usually a big deal for couples who waited.

A fairy tale wedding ended with a departure in a horse-drawn carriage, as you wave good-bye to the people you love. And as you ride off in the distance with your prince-charming you anticipate your new adventure as a wife. All the dreams of getting married and waiting until the wedding night are now here, and your life begins now. As you ride off into the sunset your thoughts drift back and forth—back to the day you met, and thoughts of what would happen the first time. For me that dream was not as I had imagined because my thoughts were threatened by a past I tried hard to forget, but could not. Having given myself away a few months prior to my wedding, there was nothing to really look forward to. We have been there and done that. The story of my wedding night had been rewritten by me months before I said I do. For me the script began with my upbringing in a conservative home which was strictly defined by the values and rules that were in place long before I was born. I'd been threatened and scared to death not to have sex before marriage.

Undoubtedly, as mentioned earlier, those fears followed me and haunted me for years until I finally decided to break the rules. All the while I knew my wedding night would be wonderful because I'd waited. Then the glorious, long-awaited night came and I was not a virgin. What was to be a great explosion of emotions became a night filled with regret of giving myself away too early. My virginity was not mine to give; it was mine to keep in waiting for my husband on our wedding night. After getting over the initial shock of my failure to maintain my virginity and the shame I felt knowing my testimony was no longer complete, I forgave myself and settled into my new life, as a wife and a mother. Waiting does suck, but you can make your wedding night awesome by waiting and experiencing new things with your husband or wife for the very first time.

#Just A Few Reasons To Wait

Waiting builds tension, the anticipation of that first night is definitely worth waiting for. When you start having sex too early, you are bound to get burnt out eventually. It's like rushing a meal too fast, and you can't really enjoy it and may get bored. When I spend $40 on a plate of sushi, I take my time to savor every bite. Sex is the same way, if you stuff yourself too fast with pleasures, you will get bored, but if you pace yourself you will savor it. None of my guy friends have ever called a girl back after a one-night stand, unless they plan to have a sexual relationship going forward.

I have watched several movies showing a woman crying in the corner of the shower scene trying to wash away the scent of a man and the mistake she made sleeping with that man. When you have sex at the wrong time with the wrong man, it is usually filled with regrets, you can always go forward, but can never go back to erase the mistakes you made. A perfect relationship can be ruined by having sex. There are so many good reasons to wait.

#What Are You Waiting For?

In life we wait for many things, we wait in line at Starbucks, at a movie theater, we wait in traffic, or wait in line at a restaurant. We all have one reason or another to wait; knowing what you are waiting for will determine how long you wait, and the reward for waiting will determine your endurance level. Most of us wouldn't mind waiting for hours to pick up a million dollar check promised to us by a random stranger. However, when it comes to sex, we find it hard to wait.

First I believe when you know what you are waiting for, it helps with making the right decisions and gives you the strength you need to say "No," when others are saying "Yes." So what are you waiting for? When you save sex for marriage, you are saving your heart from been tainted and tampered with. You are waiting for an undefiled and sacred expression of true love. You are saving yourself from diseases, and the repercussions of having a child out of wedlock.

#How Long Should You Wait?

Some people wait till after three dates, some after the first I love you, others until they are about to lose their minds, and others until their wedding night. Whatever the case, how long you wait should be a decision based on your principles. And keep in mind that sex might, and most likely will, break up a relationship or tear it apart no matter how long you wait to have sex. If you are not married to a man, there is no guarantee he will stay after having sex with you.

#Waiting For Sex. Kinda

This is what I call the Bill Clinton effect, the declassification of certain acts as not being sex. Sex as I found out, means different things to different people. When issues over sex become a big deal in your relationship or cause your relationship to fail, then that means you have given sex the power to rule in your affairs. Waiting is all about timing, and if the person you are courting does not understand that aspect of your life, then its best to let him or her go. Sex has the power to destroy a relationship, but it does not have the power to save a relationship. Waiting usually filters out the jerks, If he was not interested before, he won't be interested after you have sex with him. You may lose a guy you like, but isn't it better if that happens before having sex with him? Although some of us really would like to wait for the right person and the right time, we spend endless time pushing the envelope and crossing boundaries.

For some waiting means not having sex, while doing every other thing under the sun, while for others waiting means abstaining from all things sensual until they get married. As a teenager I believed in waiting, but progressively, I began to flirt with the idea of indulging myself in acts that seemed innocent at the time. Eventually, the more boundaries I crossed, the more I gave up my standards and fell into more sin. If you are going to wait, then truly wait. No kind of, or sort of to it; just wait.

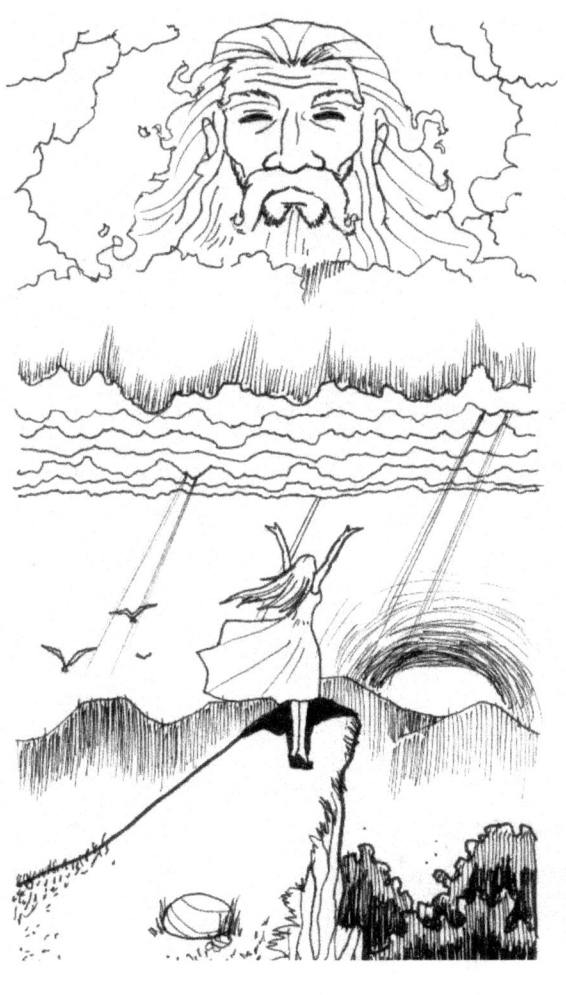

"A beautiful and chaste woman is the perfect workmanship of God, and the true glory of angels, the eare miracle of earth, and the sole wonder of the world."
— George Hermes

CHAPTER 8
Who Are You Dating?

#What Type Of Man Are You?

I love men. I love their deep voices. I love the way they think. I love their strength. I love their authority. I love their complexity. I intend to spend the rest of my life with a man. I plan to bear his children as well as build a life and develop a home with him. I would not dream these dreams if I did not love men. They are our brothers in the faith and our champions when we are unsafe. I am not suggesting that women are not capable of taking care of themselves, but it is lovely to share and grow with a wonderful man. This book is not about man bashing. It is about calling us all to a higher level of purity. It is about forgiveness and understanding.

There are problems with men and women though. These are serious problems and we have to address them if we are to grow and fulfill God's plans. Some of the problems are with women and some are with men. Let's talk about them.

THE BEGGING BOY

This is the guy that whines, needles, and begs like a never-ending squeaky wheel. He acts so desperate to be with you. He cannot live without sex. He is a man and he has needs. Please! Please! If you love me, PLEASE!

These guys make you feel like if they do not have sex with them that they might die. They are relentless and it wears you down. Honestly, I have to wonder how many girls have lost their virginity just to shut a guy up? What do we do with the begging boy? Well, my first choice is for you to get out of the relationship as fast as you can and get his voice out of your head. Maybe a kick in the shin before you run away might also do the trick. However, that is not the way of the cross.

The way of the cross is a better higher way. Pray for him; pray with a Christian leader; and seek counsel from a trusted older person. No one has ever died from celibacy; they just feel like they might. Your begging boy will survive your firm "NO." The most enduring and faithful friend I have is a man I said no to. I value him and treasure his friendship to the depths of my heart. No is not a bad word.

THE MANIPULATOR

These guys are smooth. They listen to you carefully and agree that you are on the right track. It is strange, though, how often you find yourself in a darkened room with a man that has suddenly sprouted extra arms and a flailing tongue when you really did think you were going to watch your favorite movie. Sexual situations sprout up around him like weeds and, as soon as you manage to sidestep one situation, there is another one coming. Manipulators find the things that move you—the special song that brings you to tears, the brilliant sunset that captures your imagination, and the carefully prepared story that tugs at your heartstrings.

A good way to see if these gestures are the real thing or just a troubled man's ploy to get you into a sexual situation is to look at his track record and listen to how he talks about past relationships. If he is disdainful of every girl he has dated, or if he has been dumped at every turn, be cautious.

A track record is a good tool to help you understand what may happen to you. Again, pray for this guy. Do not put yourself in situations that will test his or your limits. When he brings you home from a date and lingers over the good night hug, then take charge and move away. If you really like him, give him the opportunity to be honorable.

THE HYMEN HATER

These men have not waited and do not understand that you want to wait until marriage even if it is hard and an unpopular thing to do. They usually think that a girl that has already had sex will be easier to convince to have sex and, to be honest, they do not bother with virgins. It can be very hurtful to find a young man attractive and then realize that he really only wants to be involved with you because he thinks he will get sex from you. We all hope that a man will see that there is more to us than our sexuality and that we all have dreams. The men that I have met that have despised me because of my virginity have really broken my heart, not just because they dumped me when they found out there was not going to be any sex, but also because they are selling themselves short. If all he sees in you is the possibility of sex, then what does he see in himself? He must not believe that he has much to offer a girl besides sex as well. It is sad.

If you are unsure of yourself at all, then avoid men with this reputation at all costs because you can be terribly hurt. If you are strong and if you have a great support system, it is good to be a friend with these guys. They need to learn to be friends with women and to trust themselves to make better choices. Remember, it is not your job to save them from themselves. It is God's job. You can be a witness, but it is not up to you to sacrifice your virtue to be close to them. If it means that they will not get involved with you, then so be it. God has a plan for you and you must not forget that. Always pray for those that use you and always move forward with your life.

THE BULLY

If we are being honest, we have to admit that there are men out there who are purposely cruel and hurtful. The difficult thing to admit is that someone who is sweet to us one minute, make us feel like a princess, and acts like we are the greatest treasure on the planet can then, just as quickly, become our worst nightmare. Some bullies are very subtle and they make us believe we deserve to be treated badly. We find ourselves trying to appease them and keep them from getting angry or acting disappointed in our constant failures. Never buy into this.

Understand that people get angry at each other in relationships and, sometimes, they even lose their temper, but it is normal and there should never be any fear or violence involved in this natural experience. If you are spending all your time trying not to disappoint your boyfriend or, even worse, if you are afraid of him, seek counseling immediately and move in another direction with your life. There is no place in the Bible that teaches that women are supposed to be manipulated or beaten down by their mates. In fact, the Bible teaches that we are to be as servants to each other, building each other up in Christ. There is nothing rational about being abused or used. You are not obligated to please any man sexually outside of marriage regardless of how much he insists or pressures you.

THE GODLY MAN

Here is the one type of man that is the hardest to describe and to resist. Here is the man you will probably want to marry, mainly because he is trying as hard to live a Godly life as you are and he is struggling to remain pure just like you are. This man is difficult to describe because he comes in all shapes and sizes, and it is hard to resist him because you do truly love him. He wants the same things you want and he faces the same temptations you face. When he kisses you, it is because he loves you and when he goes too far, he feels badly about it and wants to find the best path toward your future.

It is hard to be strong when you do truly love someone and it is hard to wait. I have never met anyone that has said, "(Sob) I am so sorry I waited until after I was married!

(Sob, sob!)" On the contrary, those who wait have proven something to themselves and to God. They have proven that they are strong enough to be faithful and they have shown the Lord that they love Him enough to sacrifice momentary pleasure in favor of a lasting happiness in Christ.

#What Type Of Woman Are You?

I have to be honest and admit that it is not just the young men that are creating problems. Some of the trouble comes from the blossoming bodies of young women. Not all of our ladies have their priorities straight. If anyone is putting pressure on you to fit in, then they are not being a true friend. If your friends are telling you that it is okay to have sex before you are married, then you have to make some decisions about those friendships and stick with the decision. Are you strong enough to stand up to your friends? Be honest. Always be honest. Here are some things to consider.

THE TEASE

We all know a tease and, to be honest, they can be the most interesting, most vivacious, and the friendliest girls in the room. They flirt and are playful and they are truly fun and adventurous to be around. Unfortunately, they, sometimes, are heartbreakers, and leading anyone astray is not a good plan for salvation. In fact, it is not a reflection of Christ at all. Being a sexual daredevil is not something that glorifies God and it leaves young men with a bitter taste in their mouth. I know several young men that are different after having their hearts broken by teases. I also know several young women that have experienced terrible repercussions because of their teasing.

It often seems like what we do in our youth has no lasting consequences but that is not true. What we do with each day is important. What we learn from our studies is important even if we do not use it in our careers. This is because everything we learn builds neural connectors in our brain and makes our brain stronger. The same is true with making moral choices. Every time we choose to do the better thing, our moral fiber gets stronger. Every good choice builds our character and our future. I know the future seems very far away, but, as a thirty something year old, I have discovered that our far-off dream of "someday" is really right around the corner. What kind of woman do you intend to be? There is nothing sadder than an old party girl. I would hate to think that anyone would sacrifice their true happiness for the fleeting approval and excitement that comes with teasing.

THE GIVE-IT-UP GIRL

These young ladies really break my heart. They are so desperate to be loved and think that giving in to a boy's advances will automatically make him love them and commit to them. "I'll give you my body and you give me your heart" is no guarantee that a young man will comply with the bargain. Some guys are so desperate for sex when they are surrounded by moonlight that they will agree to anything, but, in the bright light of morning, they are much more interested in football with their friends. Be smart. If he says he loves you in the moonlight, be happy and content with that and insist he be happy and content with that. If he loves you as much when you interrupt his game of football to say good morning, then that is a sign that his feelings are real. Everyone looks better with moonlight in their eyes. Making decisions when you are full of reason indicates that you are in a real relationship.

Any spur of the moment decision that you make about sex will likely be a bad one. When someone says that they love you in the middle of making out, then that probably means that they love making out with you. I tend to believe someone really loves me when he says it with conviction and emotion, unprovoked, unasked, and unprompted by raging hormones. Do not be needy. That does not mean that needing someone is wrong. It means be satisfied with your life and be patient.

THE FRIEND PLEASER

As an emerging adult, probably one of the most difficult issues to deal with is peer pressure. As a woman that loves and values her friendships, I can say from my own experience that when your friends are having sex, it is harder to resist. We want to fit in and join in the intimate conversations and shared confidences of friendship. When my friends talked about doing it with their boyfriends and I had nothing to say, I felt left out and, to be honest, a little foolish. Maybe they were more sophisticated than I was; maybe they were more attractive than I was; and maybe I would never grow up. I did not want them to leave me behind, so it made me bolder.

We are taught to stand out in a crowd by being the best at something, but, let's face it, it is hard to be the best. Fitting in is hard enough. To stand out in a crowd by taking a moral stand really makes us a target. Sometimes, even our friends turn away from us when we take a strong moral stand. I truly hope that if this is a situation you find yourself in that you will continue to be strong and find support for your brave stand.

What is important to understand is that you have your whole life ahead of you and the friendships that are made while we are very young may or may not endure throughout your life. What does endure throughout your whole entire life is the deep abiding truth of your faith. Please God, rejoice in the higher and better things. You will meet many people in your life and, as you grow, you will find you have less of a need to fit in with your friends.

THE PEDESTAL PRINCESS

I do not really like talking about this, but I have to be honest and honesty, sometimes, is not pretty. I have met some girls that use their sexuality to get what they want from boys. Their bodies are like bargaining chips for getting what they want. They want to go to prom with a certain guy and so she bargains for the date. She wants the prestige of pretty things given to her by boys she thinks like her for herself. It is a fool's delusion. Trading sex for security, prestige, comfort, or anything is a form of selling yourself. Women who sell themselves are called prostitutes. Sex is not a bargaining chip. Sex should be as much for the woman as it is for the man, and I have rarely heard of the man getting a nice necklace for having sex. Do not sell yourself for baubles. It cheapens what should be a holy union. Integrity is as important in the bedroom as it is in the boardroom. Climb off the pedestal and stop using your sexuality as a bargaining chip. There is not enough money to buy what is given as a gift from your heart.

THE GODLY WOMAN

Hopefully, there are many more ladies reading this that see themselves in this category than in any of the other groups. This is the group that, like the Godly Man, truly tries to do the right thing. Recently, I heard about a couple that was within days of their marriage and the waiting was becoming too hard for the young woman. She was in love; she was committed; and she was ready to be a wife.

During an intimate moment, she suggested that perhaps it might be alright to consummate their relationship. To her surprise, her fiancé refused, saying they had made it this far so they could manage a few more days. She was frustrated but relieved, and on her wedding day, she wore white and it meant something special to her and to her new husband. Doing the right thing was frustrating for a night, but it was with honor and pride that she walked down the aisle. So many couples fight the urge to consummate their relationship before their wedding and they fail. I do not know what impact that has on their marriage, but I do know that a blessing was missed and, even if the lovemaking was precious, it was still out of sync with God's will. It is better to wait. God's forgiveness is there for the very human moments we experience.

*"It's bad enough that people are dying of AIDS,
but no one should die of ignorance."*
— Elizabeth Taylor

CHAPTER 9
Keeping Yourself Pure

In a world filled with people who think sex is as casual as saying hello, everyone, even a Christian, thinks engaging in premarital sex is okay. The question is: How long should a person wait before having sex? Answer: Wait until you are married. The Bible clearly states why sexual sin is bad. Yet, we try to justify this act by inventing excuses. How can you keep yourself pure in a world where the act of conquest is shown on television every day for us to see? Over the years, I have come to realize that there is nothing you can do to keep yourself pure. Only God can provide wisdom on how to live your life in purity.

Ninety-nine percent of those who wear purity rings lose their virginity. Keeping your chastity takes more than just wearing a ring or signing a vow. However, in the large scope of things, the greatest ability to stand on the ideology of purity has to come from God who ultimately will give you the strength to stand strong.

Remember that story in the Bible in which a woman by a well had experienced several sexual partners? She met Jesus and had her life changed. Living a pure life is not just for those who are virgins; it is also for those who have fallen but are trying to do the right thing. Purity is also not just for women, but it is also for men. Keeping yourself pure is important. It focuses your attention on the things that matter the most. Purity says to others that you respect yourself and that you value your body enough to wait. Therein lay integrity and character.

When I got the idea for this book, I thought I was not the best person to write a book on chastity. I was sure there were men out there, especially those I went out with in the past, who would read this and disagree about being "chaste." After a while, writing this book became a quest for self-forgiveness. I knew that I did not have the cleanest of lives, but God reminded me of all the imperfect people He used in the Bible.

Writing this book was a battle. The Devil made sure that he reminded me of my past and my mistakes, even those things I had forgotten. I am in no way qualified to write about keeping oneself pure, but God is more than qualified. He uses the foolish things of this world to show forth His glory.

Your body should be used for glorifying God and to please your husband when you finally meet him. So, if that man walks away because you do not want to sleep with him, do not worry about it. From now on, until you meet the one you will marry, do not have a sex life. Waiting for the right time is not a closet conversation; it should be something you are proud of. Whether you know it or not, your friends who had sex before or who are having sex now wish that they could be like you. Though some of you have had sex before, God can restore your virginity by purifying your thoughts and actions. It is better for you not to have a sex life. Stay away from every sexual act: masturbation, oral sex, anal sex, intercourse, fondling, cybersex, and phone sex. Be a virgin at heart even if you have lost it physically.

There will always be temptations, but God makes a way of escape. Exercise your power of self-control and be transformed by the renewing of your mind. So, if you feel like your life is ruined due to the lack of sex, remember that God has a better plan for your body. If someone wants to leave you because of not sleeping with him, then let him go. Sex is a powerful thing that should not be taken lightly. It may last only a few minutes, but its effect is eternal. Purity is a state of mind. No matter where you are now you may be a virgin; you may be struggling with lust; you may have had sex before or have trouble with impure thoughts; and you may feel a need for masturbation and pornography. However, God's grace is sufficient for you. He can heal everything in you that is not according to His will.

There is nothing wrong in knowing that you are imperfect. A lot of people out there are fighting battles every day to stay pure. Some people cannot explain why they do the things they do. Battles over sexual habits can be won through Christ. He is faithful and just, and He will save us from all unrighteousness. At times, we are bogged down with so much guilt and shame that we fail to ask God to cleanse us. However, it is essential to realize that nothing can save us except God. We were created as sexual beings and there is nothing wrong with having certain needs.

What is wrong is when we let those needs run wild inside of us and then act out our thoughts with people whom we are not married. Why chase after unprofitable pleasures? Why spend your days in the guilt and shame that comes after a mistake has been made? Why hide your face from God when He has the power to help heal your infirmities?

Spend your time asking God for the ability to wait in purity. Set your attention on career goals, educational goals, and things that can improve your life and self-esteem. Cultivate your gifts and begin to use them. Single people are advised to spend time pleasing God. Occupy your mind with things that are needful, helpful, and, most especially, pure. As the saying goes, "An idle mind is the Devil's workshop." I know that I do not have all the answers, but one thing is certain: God, who is an advocate for purity, will aid you one hundred percent and He will help you stand firm on your commitment to stay pure.

When you avoid the temptation, you are saving yourself from getting emotionally attached to someone out there that you do not truly love. You are also protecting yourself from sexual disease and, most importantly, you are saving yourself spiritually. No one ever said waiting would be easy. However, it sure beats the heartache that comes with fornication and the spiritual death that comes from trying to live with the Lord and, yet, giving in to the desires of the flesh. The battlefield is the mind. As long as Satan can keep it on your mind, he can get you to yield to the temptation. Resist the Devil and not the temptation.

#Now What?

Clearly, the race to purity can be a very daunting and tiresome one however; you must keep in mind that the race is worth running. The bible sums it up saying, "I have fought a good fight, I have finished my course, and I have kept the faith. Some versions say "I have finished my race."

There is more to life than sex, although sex is major component, especially in this day and age. Dating may have been very difficult for you and you probably do not have an impeccable record. Men may not stay as long and you are hoping to someday meet your Prince Charming who would respect your decisions and wait until you get married. Be strong and hold on.

The journey to purity does not come cheap. It takes a lot of work and commitment. When temptations come, as they will sometimes will, stay focused on your goal. Respect yourself enough to wait and re-evaluate why you want to wait. Make a decision and get accountable friends who believe in waiting. Record your progress by keeping a diary. It will not be easy. You can start over even if you have had pre-marital sex. There is always newness present through forgiveness.

As a teenager I fought the battle over my purity, and failed at the age of 27 when I gave it all away. The painful thought of trying so hard to fight the battle and finally giving it all up to a man that is not my present husband haunts me. Just a few more weeks of waiting for my God-given husband would have made my dreams come true. However, I have had to forgive myself and moved on.

Looking back all of those experiences have made me into the woman, and wife I am today. I am a better person now because I understand my weaknesses, recognize my strengths, and work on both. The length and nature of your journey cannot be determined by others—not your parents, not your church, and not your friends.

This race is within you. It starts inside of you and God is the compass. The race to purity cannot be won overnight, but it is a journey worth embarking on because, at the end, you will emerge a pure damsel exquisite in beauty with great pride in yourself and in your creator who has your life firmly pressed in the palms of His hands.

Happy Waiting!

A Single's Chic Guide To Dating And Waiting

#WAYS TO TAME YOUR FLESH

1. Pray. Every activity should begin and end in prayer. If you are struggling with a prayer about the activity, chances are you should not be doing that particular thing. Of course, that realization will certainly give you something to pray about!
2. Take a cold shower. Sometimes, something simple works.
3. Fight the urge to call your boyfriend. Call your mother instead, which is a real urge killer!
4. Get your mind off of it by reading, drawing, singing, or doing any activity that you are good at besides sex.
5. Exercise to release some tension.
6. Engage in productive activities.
7. Volunteer to help someone do a project.

#TEN THINGS TO DO WITH YOUR BOYFRIEND/DATE/FIANCEE BESIDES SEX

1. Go out in public instead of spending time alone. Go get ice cream instead of making out.
2. Go to a nice park or other public place to talk.
3. Go swimming. Again, it is great exercise and you will get healthier.
4. Cook a new recipe together.
5. Pray together.

6. Go to the gym or exercise. Take up a sport together.
7. Do volunteer work together.
8. Take care of some children together. It will help you learn about your special someone.
9. Spend time with a married couple. You will learn about life and clarify your ideas.

#FOUR PLACES TO AVOID MEETING MEN

1. Bars and clubs. Men that are going to these places are looking to party, so stop looking for love in bars and clubs!
2. Parties where there is alcohol being served.
3. Parties where the majority of people are not practicing Christians.
4. Online chat rooms. This is very risky!

#PLACES TO MEET NICE MEN

1. Weddings
2. Church
3. Work
4. School
5. Through godly friends or family
6. Volunteer work
7. Interest groups

#THINGS TO TALK ABOUT: DATING 101

Dating is an interview process that occurs either on the phone, online, or in person. It is very important to meet with a date in person because anyone can be whatever or whoever they want to be on the phone or online. First dates should be at a coffee shop, a quiet restaurant, a museum, or anywhere quiet enough to talk. Never go to your date's house or apartment on your first date unless he/she lives with his/her parents and you know for a fact they will be home.

#DATE INTERVIEWS

Below are questions to ask your date. Do not ask all of these questions on the first day. It makes you out to be a desperate person who will haul them off to the altar. Under no circumstances should you tell him you have your wedding gown in your closet and his tuxedo already ordered for that special day even if it is true. He will run as fast as his legs can carry him trust me!

This is when you should ask very important questions that will determine if you should go forward with your date or dump him. These questions are not set in stone, You should have fun with the way you ask them or you can make up your own, so be creative. I call the first date questions fat-free because they are light; hey will not weigh you and your date down. Caution: Do not ask questions like you are about to hire them for a job although we both know they are being interviewed for the most rewarding and greatest job of all time, which is to be with the most special person ever created: you.

1. Definitely get their first and last name. (Hope you know this already!)
2. Where are you from?
3. Do you have siblings? How many?
4. Find out how old they are.
5. What are their Interests? Hobbies? Passions? Dreams? (You can learn a lot by matching where you are going with their dreams.)
6. Are you a Christian? How often do you go to church?
7. Find out about their beliefs. Discover what is important to you, such as if they believe in pro-life, speaking in tongues, abstinence, tithes, offering, etc. Ask specific questions, such as: What do you think of abortion? Do you think paying ten percent of your income to a church makes sense? Ask questions to get direct answers. This is very important because this can be a determining factor on whether or not you want to continue dating this person or not, depending on what is important to you. For me, I never go out with a man that does not see anything wrong with sex before marriage. A good way to do this is to have a list that includes what your mission, your beliefs, and your visions are.
8. Do you smoke, drink, or do drugs?

9. What do you do for fun?
10. What is your view of God?
11. Ask about school and work. It is important to know if your date has goals, has a job, or goes to school. Ask if he/she went to school and how long, etc.
12. Ask about their favorite movie or music. Personally, I used this to determine a lot about a man I am trying to date. A person's movie choice can tell you a lot about their personality and moral standard.

"The Englishman can get along with sex quite perfectly so long as he can pretend that it isn't sex but something else."
— James Agate

CHAPTER 10
Stories I Heard Or Were Sent To Me Over The Years

#I Gave The Devil My Dreams On A Platter

Chants of praises ascended into the dark night as families sat under the oak tree, looking into the stars of the night. "That's my star." "No, that's my star." The little children ran around in their underwear pointing to the heaven. The percolating smell of burning firewood filled the air. I was home for the holidays and there was nothing to do but to help my father run his drug store. That was the only source of medicine in the village. My dad was an apprentice for a late missionary in the 1970s. The missionary back then had built a tiny drug store to help take care of the sick. My dad worked for him and assisted him in handing out medicines to those that were ill, treat wounds, and giving care to the sick.

After the missionary died of Malaria, my dad took over the drug store. He was known as "dokitor" meaning doctor. I started attending college to become the first real doctor in my family. So, every summer, I would come home and work for my dad.

Over the years, my dad added extra quarters to the drug store, which was equipped with five beds for overnight admissions. I was always looked upon with envy because I took charge of the facility and treated patients with the little knowledge I had gained from medical school. My dream was to take over my father's business and expand it into a big hospital after graduation. I saved up for it and spoke to everyone I met in college. I never had time for boys. I had a goal in mind. I wanted to be independent and I wanted to become a doctor.

"That's the one that is in school to become a doctor" the women said pointing to me.

"Look at her, she's so smart."

"I beg face your studies o" my aunt said in broken English. It means: "Make sure you study hard."

"Yes, ma," I smiled.

I got up and walked away to meet the other people sitting in front of my neighbor's house. There were five of them—three guys and two girls around my age. I knew four of them except one young man.

"Hello," I said to them sitting down on the mat.

"Have we met?" the young man I did not know said, shaking my hands.

Before I could get my words out, he introduced himself. "My name is Ola. I came to visit my uncle. I go to school abroad in Europe really," he gloated.

I was disgusted by the pride he displayed, but I was instantly taken by his intelligence and confidence.

"Oh, okay," I said.

I later found out that night that he was in school to become a doctor too. He attended the University of Manchester and would be graduating in a year. I told him of my dream to build a hospital in the village and to provide health care for my people. We laughed and talked for hours. I loved the way he talked and, for the first time, I started falling in love. He said I was Europe material and that he came home to find a wife and I seem like that type of woman he would love to marry. Every word he said made me blush. I melted into his eyes as we talked about life and what we wanted for the future. We got up and walked away from the crowd and I simply basked in the moment. We sat by the river bank and talked.

"It is getting chilly." I said shivering.

"Here, take this," he said handing me his sweater.

"Thanks," I said.

"I will only be here for a week and then I will return to Europe," he said.

"Oh," I replied.

"Yea, maybe you can come visit me in Lagos and then we can make plans for you to come to Europe and finish up your education," he said.

"Well, I don't even know you," I said. He moved closely to me and heat signals surged through me and I got lost in his arms and I forgot myself. I gave myself to him willingly without hesitation. He captured my heart within hours and my body was his to have. I shivered and drifted in and out of reality as I gave myself away. We met at the riverbank every night for the whole weekend and he told me I was the best he has ever had.

We talked about marriage, children, career, Europe, and life. I was on cloud nine. I decided to stay a couple of more days in the village because he said he loved me so much. I could not go with him to Lagos that Wednesday, but he promised to call me as soon as he got there. We talked every day until his plane left that Saturday from Lagos Airport. For a week, I did not hear from Ola and I prayed nothing happened to his flight. I was afraid they got in a crash or something. I visited the Internet café every day to see if he e-mailed me. I checked for stories on Yahoo to see if any plane crash occurred.

Weeks turned to months and months to a year. There was nothing from Ola. My heart was broken and I felt betrayed. I went home that summer, hoping to hear something from his uncle but nothing. No one in the village knew that I had slept with him but my parents knew of his intent to marry me. One sunny afternoon, I saw Ola's uncle sitting with his hands on his head crying. I went close to hear what was going on. My dad sat down with him, consoling him and shaking his head.

"Who died?" I asked.

A plunging fear gripped me as millions of thought raced down my mind.

"Ola is dead," he said. "My daughter I am so sorry," he said again.

I felt like dying a thousand deaths as I fell on the floor.

"What killed him?" I asked.

"He was sick for months and they later found out he had AIDS. It was so far gone that they could not treat it."

"A-I-D-S." My tongue was tied. I stood up and started walking towards my room. Hands holding my abdomen, I felt like throwing up. "Ola died of AIDS," I said repeatedly. "Oh, my God," I screamed.

At that moment, I knew I had caught the virus. It explained a lot, my sickness, my rapid weight loss, everything. I tested positive for AIDS and started the treatments. The money I had been saving to build my hospital was now being used for medication to keep me stable. Those women still point to me in the village; but this time around they do it with disgust. "That's the doctor's daughter that caught AIDS."

"Make Una run from her, Oh, make Una no let 'em touch your pikin. Run away from her. Don't let her touch your children." I have been stigmatized by my disease and my dad's business has collapsed. Most people would rather walk thirty kilometers to get their medicine. They treat our family like outcasts and will not even use the drug store anymore. I hated myself for having sex without using protection. I have handed my life and dreams on a platter to the Devil and now I have lost everything. Do not let one moment of pleasure rob you of your dreams and future. Your actions may not only affect you, but they will also

touch your loved ones too. I wish I waited and was patient enough to know the guy better. I was so quick to fall for the lies he painted so well.

If you have never had sex, please wait and, if you have in the past, start over and try to wait. Protect yourself, protect your heart, and protect your dreams. I wish I had protected mine.

– Kemi, A.

#My One-Night Stand Baby

At that age of twenty, I never knew that I would be having my first child, becoming another number on the roster of government statistics. I never had dreams of waiting until marriage. I thought it was ridiculous.

There is nothing wrong with sex, and yes, I still believe that. The problem is when you have sex with the wrong person at the wrong time. You subject yourself to heartache, physical scars, and spiritual bankruptcy.

Now, I am carrying a child who is a product of a one-night stand with a guy I met at the club. I had a lot of one-night stands in the past and nothing bad ever happened. I protected myself and used the proper precautions. This quickie, though, was different. The condom broke and he did not even say a word.

A month later, I missed my period. I went to the school clinic where the two little pink lines changed the course of history for me. I scrambled to find his number in my little black book—the little black book that holds the names and number of every guy I have ever slept with. I had little shorthand codes by the names that only I understood. "GX" was for good sex; "BX" was for bad sex; "WDIA" stood for will do it again if need be; "BS" was for best sex ever; and "ONS" stood for one-night stands. Six guys graced that page—from Kevin that I met at a friend's party to Deon, the "BS" I had ever had to Ted, my baby's daddy. I dialed his number with hands shaking.

"Hello, may I speak to Ted?" I asked.

"Who is this?" he said.

"Um!!! You probably don't remember me, but my name is Alicia and we met at the club, Hypnotized, last month."

"So, what can I do for you?" he asked.

"Well, remember we slept together that night at your place?"

"Am I supposed to keep track of every female I sleep with?" he said. "So what do you want?" he asked.

"I am pregnant with your baby." I said, somehow hoping he would jump for joy.

"I don't even remember you!" he yelled.

Before I could say anything else, he hung up the phone. I wept and I felt so embarrassed by the situation. I knew that I could not get rid of the baby, but I wished I could take that night back. I am now eight-months pregnant and Ted only contacted me once. I do not blame him and, in some ways, I am glad he is not part of my life. I would be stuck with a deadbeat father who knows nothing about me and could care less about me and my baby.

I had to face my family and tell them I was pregnant. That was not the plan I had for my life, but I guess I have to roll with the punches and still make something out of my life. When you are told to wait, it is not to deprive you of having fun; it is to preserve you and keep you from making mistakes that may affect your future.
– Alicia (St. Louis)

#My Secret Sex Life

I am a minister in a local church. I teach teenagers about abstinence and I am considered a role model among my peers. I have had to put up the good girl image for so long that I felt trapped by it. Every so often, I would cling to the notion that if I were to fail being a good girl that I would fail in everything. My life depended on my good girl image.

I was the good church girl on Sundays, but I lived a different life during the week. I am addicted to sex. I love sex, but I am a natural born actress to the extent that you would not be able to tell that I had a double life.

I told the girls that I mentor that I was a virgin. I told my church boyfriend that I was a virgin, but, on the contrary, I had a sex life and a very active one at that. I slept with anyone that gave me attention and used sex as a way to get validation. I have really tried to practice what I preach but to no avail. I figured having sex with a guy would make the guy love me. I would give a guy oral sex so that he would be happy with me. Usually, that would last for a while, but then he would break up with me and I would move on to another man, hoping that things would be different. I have been going around in circles, trying to figure out what happened to me and how I got like this.

Last week, I realized that my problem is a lack of self-esteem. I do not truly love myself and I thought opening my legs for a man would make him love me. I was wrong. I had to come clean to not just anyone but to God and myself. I realized that I had been attracting the wrong set of men into my life because of the lack of self-worth I had for myself. Those men cannot give me what I could not even give myself. Instead of feeling condemned, I decided to look for things to replace sex in my life. I started writing poetry. That has really helped me a lot. I transmuted my sexual energy into writing about my feelings.

I am beginning to have a positive self-image about myself and I do not need a man to validate me. My secret life is not so secret anymore because I have shared my experiences with the teens in my class. They now are more open with me and are able to share their struggles with me. It has been great to know that I was not the only one with a secret sex life. Talking about it has helped me stay grounded and I now have tons of people reading my life as if it were a book.

– Tiffany, B. (Bradenton, Florida)

#The Good Girl

I had the worst date ever. There was this guy in my engineering class. He was so intelligent, looked good, and had been flirting with me since the first day of class. He finally asked me out and I was so excited. We went to the movies that night. After the movies, we went outside to wait for the cab. While we were waiting, he asked if he could kiss me. I said yes. I leaned forward to kiss him and, as we made out, he pulled me to the corner of the movie theater and lunged at me with full force. I hesitated but gave in eventually. We began making out for what seemed like an eternity when we heard a voice from the corner. It was the cab driver. I was so embarrassed and, after that night, we never spoke again. I caught him pointing to me in class and laughing with his fraternity brothers. I felt so bad because I have tried hard to live up to this good girl image and I feel like I just messed it all up. How do I explain to him that I am not that kind of girl?

Professing a good girl image and living a good girl image are two different things. You can profess to be good but be the complete opposite. You can also try to be good but fall short. In my case, I believe I am a good girl who happened to make a bad choice. If a man makes out with you in public without regards to the public, then he does not care about you. You have only known this guy for a few weeks and have only gone out with him once. He probably is that kind of guy—the one that loves a quick fix. Do not feel bad because you made a mistake. It happens to everyone. I realize I do not owe him an explanation. I know who I am regardless of my mistakes. I have to love myself, ignore him, and move on.

– Sarah, K. (Louisville, Kentucky)

#Detour! Sex Ahead

We met in church. He was in the choir and I was the usher. We were both sophomores in college and, after a few dates; I really started to like him. He introduced me to his parents. He wanted us to pray about marriage and God's will. The first time I went to his apartment, I noticed a lot of female pictures, but I did not think too much about it. I noticed a lot of the movies he rented for us to watch had a lot of sex scenes in it. It was a little disturbing at first but I also ignored it. We would make out at his apartment. He would touch me and then apologize. After a while, we began crossing the boundaries we had set in the beginning of our courtship. I really did not want to do all of those things, but we were engaged to be married.

It was the day after Christmas when it happened and it is one that I wish I could forget. It lasted for about five minutes on the floor in his apartment. There was no queen-size bed, no rose petals, and no breakfast in bed the next morning. Tears poured down my face as I wanted so bad to wake up from the dream. But, as I drove home, I realized it was not a dream. It was real and I had just lost my virginity. It seemed like forever before I got home. I could not stop the feeling of guilt. I lied to myself that everything will be okay; we would be married in a year. He did not even call the next day. When I called him, he said he was busy working on project that was due at the beginning of the year. I saw him on Sunday while he sang in the choir, but he acted like nothing happened.

After church, he spent most of his time talking to the girls in the choir. He just waved at me and did not come to say hello. I could not even tell anyone what happened to me. By the end of the year, we were no longer engaged. I found out that my baby was arriving in August. He left the church soon after I told him and claimed that it was not his child. I was a virgin, but I acted foolishly. There were no satin sheets, no roses, and no wedding ring sitting on the bedside desk. He did not even call the day after. Please make that detour when you feel that your mind may lose control over you body.

– Gina, T. (Houston, Texas)

#The Sweetness Of Sin

I had wanted to save myself for marriage because that was the noblest thing to do. I wanted to please my family, especially my mom because she saved herself for marriage. I attended an all- girl's Catholic school in Nevada and most of my classmates were doing the same.

In 11th grade, I met Christy. She was full of life, looked innocent, and was so intelligent. At the end of the school year, we had already become close friends. Autumn rolled by with its calmness and the excitement of graduating filled the air like the smell of rain. My parents decided to move to California because my dad got a job with IBM and had to take it. So they got me an apartment close to campus and I loved it. My very own spinster's pad was decked out with nice leather furniture, a queen-size bed, a fully equipped kitchen that I never used, and a nice Jacuzzi. Christy was thrilled as we spent most of our time together in the apartment, having sleepovers, and just being crazy. By January of our senior year, Christy practically moved into my apartment because her parents lived about thirty miles away from campus. I admired Christy because she was beautiful and green, starry eyes. She loved her body so much that she would walk around nude while at my apartment. I did not have a problem with nudity and I was comfortable with her choice of expression.

A snowstorm kept us in one Friday and the school was closed for the day because of the snowstorm. We had enough groceries so we decided to cook breakfast. We watched movies, drank hot cocoa, and doubled up on the marshmallows. It was great. At about 9.00p.m., we decided to move the mattress to the living room by the fireplace and watch "Boomerang," my all-time favorite movie. I loved the whole boomerang idea of loving something, losing it, and it coming back to you. My dad bought me a boomerang from his last visit to Australia and I carried it with me everywhere. We snuggled close to each other like we always did, but, this time, something was different. Christy stroked my hair and placed her head on my shoulders and stared at me. I felt my heart skip a beat as she held me.

"It's so cold," she said sighing.

"The heat is on," I said.

I could not understand this overwhelming feeling that overtook me and I was looking at my best friend like I would a man and it scared me. I inched away from her and continued watching the movie. We fell asleep and suddenly I woke up to the taste of Christy lips on mine. It was intense and it was forbidden, but I didn't stop her. Fire surged through me as I could not help but let sin overtake my mind. We basked in the sweetness of sin and we looked at each other completely captured by lust and taboo.

The next day, we acted like nothing happened and went about our daily chores. We did not even talk about it. I wallowed in my shame and pleaded to God for redemption.

"I am not a lesbian," I kept reaffirming to myself.

When night fell, we did it again and again. We never talked about it and, after graduation, I moved to California to go to college. We kept in touch and I started dating. My thirst to prove my heterosexuality compelled me start having sex. I started engaging in acts that I never thought I would ever do. I figured sex with a lesbian was not sex as I gave in to sexual acts to prove something to myself; I started having intercourse with my boyfriend. I enjoyed sex. I loved it and could see no reason why I should not enjoy the bliss it brings. Sex was like freedom to me—a way to self-express—and the only thing I felt I could offer. I would go to church and pray to stop having sex but I could not stop myself. I really tried, but the harder I tried, the more I gave in. The energy to have sex surged through me like a mighty rushing volcano. I could not stop it.

I never told a soul about my encounter with Christy until now. I am trying to start over and reclaim my body and give God my sexuality because He created it. I met a wonderful man, a Christian man, who shared with me the power of redemption and starting over. I decided to share with him my past and he is so understanding. I clearly believe he is heaven sent and he recently proposed to me.

We both are waiting until our wedding night to have sex and it has been great having something to look forward to. I called up Christy and we forgave each other for stealing each other's innocence. For both of us, it was a release. I confessed my sins and asked God to forgive and I do believe He has. I decided to start over and reclaim my body. You can too.

Jane, H. (California)

#My Stolen Innocence

It has been six months and I can still smell him. Not a million soaps could wash his scent away from my body. For days, I sat in the shower, scrubbing, weeping, and blaming myself for going out with Tim. I should have known he would take it from me. I could not tell anyone—not even my parents.

For months, I had emotional outbursts. I was depressed and had to take a semester off to just work at the local YMCA. My body was broken. I was humbled by a man who could care less. How would I explain to my future husband what happened? Could I still consider myself a virgin? Then I started searching for answers. I went for counseling to start my healing process. It has been hard to start dating again but I am trying. I fear intimacy and cannot seem to trust anyone.

It was not my fault that I got date raped but, for a while, I thought it was. No one has the right to take your virginity. It should be given freely. I forgave Tim in my heart and started a program for ladies dealing with date rape issues. You do not have to be a victim forever. Get help and speak to someone right away. Let God heal every scar and be willing to let go of hurt. Just because someone raped you does not mean that you are no longer a virgin. Until you willingly give away that gift, you remain a virgin. Although physical evidence of your virginity may not be present, you can still be a virgin. The hymen cannot be a testament of chastity; an intact or perforated hymen does not define you. You define yourself by your own standards, and remember that stolen innocence can be restored.

Mine was and yours can too.

Kelly, G. (Lakeland, FL)

#The Pure Heart

I met Gary at the library and the connection was unspeakable. We exchanged numbers and, within days, we were out on our first date. Gary was a church boy. He loved God and played the drums for his uncle's church. By summer, he asked me to be his girlfriend and we started hanging out more often. He gave me the keys to his apartment and some of my things were there. We both set sexual boundaries early in our relationship. All we did was kiss and Gary was a disciplined young man. His relationship to God was very important and so was mine. After about six months of dating, things got a bit serious. I started spending the night at his apartment and we would lie on his bed.

At first, we would cuddle all night and wake up feeling proud of ourselves. Then, things got a lot more complicated. I would cry and we both would pray for God's forgiveness and promise not to do it again. Gary loved me so much and I loved him too, but the things we were doing started putting a strain on our relationship. We fought more and we would break up at least every other month and then get back together. We came close to having sex numerous times.

There were times I that I could not even tell people I was a virgin, especially when Gary was around. I felt like a hypocrite and like I was lying to others and myself. It is one thing to lie to others, but it is another thing to lie to yourself. Gary stood firm though and believed that God would forgive us. We would pray together and cry together. He had the heart of a child and he was pure. He helped me stay grounded and still helped save me from totally giving in.

We decided to break up and see if that helped. The next man I met was so insensitive and did not care. He just wanted to take it and have sex with me by all means. He never apologized for crossing the line and never thought what we were doing was wrong. He was not pure in heart like Gary. After four months, Gary and I got back together.

I figured it was inevitable to feel the type of passion we felt for each other. We were made for each other and connected within our soul and spirit. Our bodies only wanted to display what out souls felt. So, we decided to get married.

I will be graduating in May and Gary got a great job with a record label doing promotions. He still plays for the church and will be doing his trial sermon this Sunday to become a youth minister. We both have learned a lot through this experience and we are grateful that God preserved me. I am so glad that I still have something to save for our wedding night. I do regret the moments crowded with passion and what that did. We have seen each other naked and have done so much but God is restoring us. I try not to spend nights with Gary and, if need be, I lay on the bed while he stays on the couch. We decided to even save our kisses for the wedding day. I hope the anticipation of that helps make everything new. It is possible to start over even if you have failed in any way.

Sometimes, boundaries are hard to keep and it is okay if we mess up. You can learn a great lesson from those experiences. The good thing is the fact that Gary was on the same page as me. He wanted me to save myself and he wanted to save himself for me too. I mistook our occasional mishaps as a sign that we were not meant to be together, but a lot of singles go through this every day. I have learned a lot and I thank God because He brought the right person into my life to help preserve me. If I had stayed with the other man, I would not be where I am today. God has restored me and I can proudly consider myself a virgin. When I remember those days when my heart was so broken from giving in to lust and when I would not even pray to God or feel condemned, I smile because God has got me all the while. I just could not see it then but I do now.

Amaris, H. (Maryland)

#No, No, For My Virginity

Have you ever had a guy break up with you for not giving it up? He just stopped calling after you told him you are saving yourself for marriage? Well, that happened to me last month. I really try to avoid telling people about my sexual status. When I did in the past, people looked at me like I had a disease that was incurable. I gave this guy the privilege of knowing me and I told him my secret. I thought he was different but I was wrong. He laughed at me as we chatted over a plate of filet mignon at my favorite restaurant.

"You can't be serious," he said. "What's wrong with you?" he said dropping his utensils on the plate. "So, you mean you never did it?" He raised his eyebrow looking intense as if he was hoping to get a different answer. My heart sank. I had no different answer. He went on, "What's a pretty girl like you doing saving yourself for marriage? So, are you one of them gals who try to trap a man into marrying you if he pops that cherry, huh? For real, tell me the truth." He smiled, "You joking right? 99.9% of the girls in LA are whores, so what make you different, Virgin Mary?"

I withdrew into myself and did not speak for the rest of the night. After our date, he dropped me at home and gave me a kiss on the forehead. "Can I do that?" he asked sarcastically. "Virgin Mary, girl, you tripping." He laughed. "If you are ready to give it up, call me." He walked away popping his collar. He got into his car and left.

How humiliating. My virginity is definitely ruining my sex life. I know pre-marital sex is wrong, but I just want to know what it feels like to be intimate with a guy without the whole complicating sex things. I am so proud of the self-control I possess, being able to keep myself for this long. I am twenty-six-years-old and half of my classmates from high school are married with kids. Some are single mothers; some are in a monogamous relationship with no hopes of marriage but with an active sex life; some are bed hoppers; some are one-night standers; and then I am the almighty, no-man having, Virgin Mary. I am lonely and cannot even enjoy my own company. I feel bad when my friends are out and about. I want to be able to keep a man too.

I am beginning to think I will die alone on my porch in my house with a picket fence calling my dogs my children. I have every book ever written on the single life and satisfaction. I watch movies that speak to my emotions and cry when two people fall in love. I long to be loved and I am not afraid to admit that I am waiting for Prince Charming. My virginity means a lot to me and I have been bound to a vow to save myself for this prince of mine.

Losing my virginity before marriage is like death—not a physical death but a spiritual death. I am not doing it for just anyone and not even because the Bible says so, but I am doing it because it empowers me. It is that one thing I can save for myself and give to whomever I so choose. Although I was hurt by the comments of a non-chalant man, I chose to move forward and decided that he will not stop me from letting anyone know that I would not give it up until marriage.

Virgin Mary (Arizona)

#I Am Complete

At an early age, I decided that purity would be a choice for me in life. I learned about self-respect and self-discipline in a Sunday school lesson and I embraced that. By abstaining from sexual activity, ignoring unhealthy images of women in the media, and refusing to settle for low-quality friends, I have less pressure to be sexually active. I really enjoy living a life that is not controlled by anything but my obedience to God. I have found independence and freedom beyond belief. I live a very healthy life now and I encourage others to choose health in their lives every day.

I once dated a young man who was the picture of Christianity. He appeared to be saved, had Christian parents—his dad was a minister—and he was extremely polished and handsome. However, he was very weak in his purity walk. He constantly tried to manipulate, persuade, and coerce me into sexual sin. I stayed in the relationship because I was so happy to have a boyfriend. I felt a lot of guilt and shame in this relationship. Shame and guilt are feelings that are not of God, so I knew I had to make a change. I mustered enough energy to leave the relationship and, the more I learned about my authentic identity in Christ, the stronger I became.

I now serve as an empowerment coach to individuals and teach them about being empowered to make healthy choices in relationships. I encourage individuals to learn their identity in Christ in a solid way so that they will not be moved, or wavered, by any influence from society, friends, or the media. I have learned to love God the way I once yearned to love men. Deuteronomy 6:5 teaches to love God with all your heart (deepest devotion), your soul (what you think and what you feel), and your might (your strength and energy). I love that I am complete in Christ who is the head of all principality and power, according to Colossians 2:10. I have learned a lot from my experiences. I recognize healthy Christ-filled men when I see them. I thank God for them as well because they are proof that good Christ-filled men still exist. I choose freedom from sexual sin and I embrace that every day of my life.

Lee Felicia (The Renaissance Woman)
Motivational Speaker, Radio Show Host, and Life Empowerment Coach

#How Big Are Your Baggages?

Many people look for someone to develop a relationship

with without first developing a relationship with themselves.

Down at a church on the west side, Tommy met Mary. She was very beautiful and, right after the benediction; Tommy nervously asked to speak to Mary. At first, Mary, who was a regular member at that church, could not believe the early converted Tommy was trying to talk to her. She had an inkling of what it might be about, but she refused to make quick judgment. Mary was a lovely girl. She had a knack for working with the children in church. Her voice was also so pure that the whole church was in awe when she sang.

As soon as Tommy approached her, there was that smile on his face. "Hi Mary, I enjoyed your solo today. You have such a nice voice." "Thank you," she said. Before the compliment went any further, she proceeded to find out if he enjoyed the service. There was a long conversation on the pastor's message and the scriptures. "Yea, Mary, I was wondering if I could invite you to a cook-out on Saturday."

"Saturday, isn't that the sixth? Ummm, I think I should be able to," she nodded and smiled.

"Great! I'll pick you up at 3:00p.m. Here's my number in case you need to call me."

She replied, "All right see you later."

Saturday came and the cook-out was good. Tommy's friends thought Mary was nice, and the next weekend, Tommy took her out to a restaurant. That began their relationship. At first, everything was very nice. They were both in love with each other. But two months down the road, Tommy noticed that something was missing. Mary had very a bad temper and negative attitude. That was not the girl Tommy met a couple of months ago. She was always complaining about how she looked, her waist, her hair, everything. Tommy could not understand how a girl that beautiful would put herself down so much. Every chance she got, she pushed Tommy away. No matter how much he told her he loved her, she would not believe him. Mary went from temper tantrum to low self-esteem, emotional breakdowns, and depression. Tommy could not understand, but he was always there to pick up the pieces.

Eventually, Tommy's love was not strong enough to deal with it all. The girl he loved had evolved into this emotional wreck he did not know. On Sunday, she was all smiles and, then after the service, she was always complaining, crying and irritable. It did not work out between them and there Mary was, broken down once more, an emotional wreck, trying to pick up the pieces of her heart again. And into another relationship she went carrying her weight with her. This story basically tells us that Mary had a lot of baggage from family or past relationships even though she wore a happy face in places like church. She was completely a mess inside and every relationship Mary went into ended broken, bringing her lower than before.

The truth is that there are lots of people like Mary, walking around today in church and out of church. They do not trust anyone and they cannot trust anyone. They cannot accept love because they cannot love themselves.

Emotionally, they are dead. They have been used, abused, and victimized by the state of low esteem. Ideally, we have been taught not to sweat in public. Parents tell the boys not to cry and the girls to always have a smiley happy face. What Tommy never saw was the girl who came from a broken home, a girl who was abused at thirteen by her step father, and a girl who started having sex at fifteen. He did not see the girl who was dumped by those guys after they slept with her and a girl whose daddy left her at five and never brought the doll he promised her. He did not understand a girl that hated her face; that wished that she could look like somebody else; and that secretly hoped that her body would change overnight. She wished she were more popular, articulate, and outspoken. She never appreciated her achievements.

All of this was covered with a smile and a nice gesture of hello and hugs. Tommy and every other guy she went out with never knew this. They never asked and she never said. She secretly wished for someone to talk to, but she felt like they would run away. Sometimes, we walk around carrying issues from our past rather than fully walking in the present. Somehow, we have destroyed our relationships because we had too much of a load to carry.

Everybody has one thing or the other they are dealing with—mistakes from the past or regrets—but we need a weight limit. No baggage is recommended, but if there is any, then it should not be so much that it destroys both you and your relationships. Just because you were hurt before does not mean you will be hurt again. Just because your stepfather abused you does not mean that all men are monsters. Just because your first boyfriend dogged you out does not mean all men have no respect for women. So, here is a lesson to learn that we all need to love ourselves; take our entire burden to God; and share how we feel with a trusted friend. You will feel much better if you do. Take some time to write down those things that make you feel the way you do. Write down how you would like to feel. Examine yourself to see if you are in a healthy relationship.

Workbook

Check Him Out!

1. **Dump him or keep him?**
    a. He wants to wear your clothes.
    b. He is always bothering you about sex.
    c. He tells you it is okay if you do other stuff.
    d. He honors his mother.
    e. He tells you everybody does it.
    f. He feels bad after going too far.
    g. He runs down his ex-girlfriends all the time.
    h. He can be playful without being sexual.
    i. He acts embarrassed when you are around his friends.
    j. He wants to wait and shows his respect for your choice.
    k. He honors your curfew.
    l. He wants you to move in with him.
    m. He flirts with your friends.
    n. When the heat is on, he knows when to stop.
    o. He wants you to have phone sex with him.

2. **How do you feel about not having sex?**
    a. You feel like the world will be over soon if you do not get rid of your virginity.

b. You feel like a freak or a weirdo.
c. You feel maybe the reasons why you are not doing it is because you are ugly.
d. You are scared.
e. Your religion forbids it.
f. Your parents forbid it.
g. You have not had the opportunity.
h. You feel good about waiting and you feel in control of your life because it is your personal choice backed with inner conviction.

Reflect on your answer and pray about it. Write down your answer and ask yourself why. If your answer is from "a-c," check yourself. Waiting should not be something to be ashamed of and it should not be because you feel ugly. If it is from "d-f," check yourself too because waiting should not be something you do because someone told you to; it should be a personal decision based on your inner conviction and choice. If your answer is "h," then you are on the right path.

NOTES:

Prayer: Grant that I may never be of the occasion to drag others into hell by suggestive words, the way I dress, or through my lifestyle. Help me to be an example in word and deed. Help me to live a life of total purity. Give me the grace to turn aside from sin, no matter what the cost, so that, one day, I may be able to stand blameless. Amen

3. **What will your wedding night be like?**
    a. Like an explosive bomb and you are scared silly. (Because you lied you waited)

b. Earthquake and tears of regret.
c. Excitement and joy because you waited for him.
d. Taunting thoughts of all those men you slept with.
e. A renewed purity and the feeling of newness and redemption.
f. Better than any of your dreams.
g. Awkward but sweet.
h. I do not have a clue.

Prayer: Teach me, Lord, to live a life of total purity. Instill a real respect for purity. I entrust the purity and safety of my future spouse to your care. Help me to live a holy life so that others may see in me a reason to change their ways and that I may have the courage to resist any temptation for sinful conduct. Let others be led closer to Jesus by my example. Amen.

4. **How pure are you?**
   - Have you masturbated before? (Y/N)
   - Have you mutually masturbated before? (Y/N)
   - Have you given or received oral sex before? (Y/N)
   - Have you had anal sex? (Y/N)
   - Have you had phone sex? (Y/N)
   - Have you had cybersex? (Y/N)
   - Have you used sex toys before? (Y/N)
   - Have you been fondled or fingered before? (Y/N)
   - Have you started over and claimed the forgiveness of God? (Y/N)

If you have done all or some of these things, then this is the time to meditate and pray to God for a renewal of purity.

Prayer: You, oh Lord, are my first love and all other love should be based on you. Give me the grace to cease from toying with sin and help me to remember that my body is the temple of the living God. Help me to respect my boyfriend, or date, and help me to see him with your eyes and respect his body enough to not defile it. I entrust the purity and safety of my future spouse who I do not know yet, but God does, to your care and prayers. Teach me the value and dignity of sexual purity. Amen.

5. How far have you gone?
   a. You went out on a date and you kissed and then you called it a night.
   b. You invited him into your apartment and then you kissed and made out.
   c. You made out, your clothes came off, and you gave or received oral sex.
   d. You had intercourse.
   e. All of the above.
   f. None of the above.

If your answer is between "a-e," pray to God to forgive you and renew you. Write down how this answer makes you feel.

Prayer: Jesus, help me to love as you do. Make me pure of body, pure of mind, and pure of heart that I might see God and enjoy his plan for me. Make me clean and heal me from the wounds of sin. Strengthen me each day to live in holiness. I am weak and my heart is not pure, but, in you, I can be strong and holy. I want to have your courage to guard the purity of others and myself. Please help me in my walk with Jesus, so that I can glorify God in my body. Amen.

Scripture Reference: 1 Corinthians 6:18-20

"Flee from sexual immorality. All other sins a man commits are outside his body, but he who sins sexually sins against his own body. Do you not know that your body is a temple of the Holy Spirit, who is in you, whom you have received from God? You are not your own; you were bought at a price. Therefore honor God with your body."

These activities are for reflection purposes and it gives you a chance to really think about your choices.

6. If you could write your life's story in brief, what would it look like? Write down a summary...

_____
_____
_____
_____
_____
_____
_____
_____
_____
_____
_____
_____
_____
_____
_____
_____

7. Why do feel you are ready for sex?
_____
_____

8. Sex to me is:
_____
_____

9. To wait or not to wait? Give reasons why you would wait or not wait?
_____
_____

10. Are you holding out or are you indulging? (Y/N)
    (Take a few minutes and try to be honest with yourself. Yes, that includes making out!)

Prayer: Lord, I give my life to you; Lead me down the right path. Help me to stay away from sin and help me to desire purity. I give my life to you and my purity gives me the courage to resist any temptation for sinful conduct. Let others be led closer to Jesus by my example. Amen.

Scripture Reference: Matthew 5:28

"But I tell you that anyone who looks at a woman lustfully has already committed adultery with her in his heart."

Scripture Reference: Colossians 3:5

"Put to death, therefore, whatever belongs to your earthly nature: sexual immorality, impurity, lust, evil desires and greed, which is idolatry."

11. **Take a few minutes to think back to the first time**

you learned about sex and write down your thoughts and how that has shaped your attitudes towards sex.

_____

_____

_____

12. What have you learned about sex and virginity from reading this book?

_____

13. Has your concept about purity changed?

_____

14. How have you defined yourself in the past based on your sexual history or lack of it?

_____

15. How would you define yourself now?

_____

16. What myths are you bound to and how can you unlearn those myths and move on to the truth? How have these myths shaped your attitudes towards sex?

_____

_____

_____

17. **Do you have attainable boundaries? Set some today.** *(Examples Minimum: Holding hands; Maximum: Hugging/Peck on the Cheek. Minimum: Hugging/Peck on the Cheeks; Maximum: Kissing)*

_____
_____
_____

18. **What is the ideal thing to do and say when you are being pressured into having sex?**

_____

19. **When is the best time to tell a date that you are waiting?**
    a. In the heat of the moment.
    b. On the first date.
    c. When you are alone in his apartment on the couch making out.
    d. The instant you lay eyes on him.
    e. When you meet his mother.
    f. In front of his friends.
    g. When you are talking on the phone.
    h. When you are eating out and his mouth is full so he cannot say anything.
    i. When you are in the car before your date.
    j. When he has just pulled into the make out spot.
    k. When your clothes are off.

l. When your father makes you say it.
m. None of the above.
n. All of the above.

Scripture Reference: Deuteronomy 30:16

"For I command you today to love the LORD your God, to walk in his ways, and to keep his commands, decrees and laws; then you will live and increase, and the LORD your God will bless you in the land you are entering to possess."

Scripture Reference: 2 Chronicles 7:14

"If my people, who are called by my name, will humble themselves and pray and seek my face and turn from their wicked ways, then will I hear from heaven and will **forgive** *their sin and will heal their land.*

Create a date shopping list.

Before you decide to go out with anyone, you have to create a date shopping list so you know exactly what you are looking for before you go out with them. Now, create a date shopping list. Refer to this list before you go out with anyone.

Include physical attributes, character, race, religion, educational background, job, status, and hobbies, etc. Remember to add whatever is important to you. You know what you need; no one can come up with a list for you.

Closing Words from Vivian Elebiyo

To the reader:

Some of the stories in this book are pure fiction. They are just examples. Not all of them are based on specific people or occurrences. Any character similarities are pure coincidences. Some sections of this book illustrate my own personal stories with fictitious names for those involved. (I hope my parents do not read this!). I hope you have enjoyed this book and read more about our community projects and events on my website, which will have more books that will enlighten you. Contact us to bring the Esteemed (YOU)th Project to your teens and young adult. We are on this journey together and I hope and pray that we press on and stay focused on the destination. I hope you had a great ride.

Best Regards,
Vivian Elebiyo Okojie

To correspond with Vivian Elebiyo Okojie or for information on booking her for a speaking engagement, please e-mail her at:
info@vivianokojie.com

Or, log on to her websites at:
www.esteemedlife.org
www.vivianokojie.com
www.facebook.com/vivianelebiyo
or follow me on Twitter #vivianspeaks

This book and other products are available online and at bookstores near you.
You can also purchase a copy from
www.vivianokojie.com
and
www.elevivpublishinggroup.com

Glossary

Anal sex – a form of human sexual behavior. While there are many sexual acts involving the anus, anal cavity, sphincter valve and/or rectum, the term *anal sex* is often restricted to *anal intercourse*, which is the insertion of the erect penis into the rectum.

Ahsewo – a Yoruba word for prostitute.

Cybersex – computer sex, Internet sex, or net sex, which is a virtual sex encounter in which two or more persons connect remotely via a computer network and send one another sexually explicit messages that describe a sexual experience. It is a form of role-playing in which the participants pretend they are having actual sexual relations. Sometimes, cybersex includes real life masturbation.

Hymen – (name for the Greek God of marriage and weddings, *Hymenaeus*; later, also the Greek word for membrane; also called *maidenhead*) a fold of mucous membrane which surrounds, or partially covers, the external vaginal opening. It forms part of the vulva or external genitalia.

Masturbation – sexual stimulation, especially of one's own genitals often to the point of orgasm, which is performed manually, by other types of bodily contact (except for sexual intercourse), by use of objects or tools, or by some combination of these methods.

Non-penetrative sex (NPS) – also known as outercourse, this is sexual activity without vaginal, anal, and oral penetration. The terms, mutual masturbation and frottage, are also used but with slightly different emphasis. NPS and outercourse are rather new and not generally accepted terms, which is why some subsumed practices usually are still called "intercourse." Interfemoral intercourse and genital rubbing, although forms of outercourse, can carry a risk of pregnancy through transfer of the sperm-bearing fluids to the sex organs as well as can pose a risk of sexually-transmitted diseases if any bodily fluids are deposited on wounds or mucous membranes, such as those of the sex organs or anal membranes.

Mutual masturbation – rubbing of each other's genitals.

Nigeria – officially named the Federal Republic of Nigeria is a country in West Africa and the most populous country in Africa. Nigeria shares land borders with the Republic of Benin in the west; Chad and Cameroon in the east; and Niger in the north.

Okun – Before the abolition of the slave trade, some Yoruba groups were known among Europeans as *Akú*, a name derived from the first words of Yoruba greetings, such as *Ẹkú ààro?* 'good morning' and *Ẹkú alẹ* 'good evening.' A variant of this group is also known as the "Okun" with Okun also being a form of "A ku." These are Yoruba's found in parts of the states of Kogi—the "Yagba", Ekiti, and Kabba.

Oral sex – consists of all sexual activities that involve the use of the mouth, which may include the use of the tongue, teeth, and throat to stimulate genitalia. Cunnilingus refers to oral sex performed on a woman and fellatio refers to oral sex performed on a man. Analingus refers to oral stimulation of a person's anus.

Phone sex – a type of virtual sex that refers to sexually explicit conversation between two or more persons via telephone, especially when at least one of the participants masturbates or engages in sexual fantasy. Phone sex conversation may take many forms, including (but not limited to): guided, narrated, and enacted suggestions; sexual anecdotes and confessions; candid expression of sexual feelings or love; discussion of very personal and sensitive sexual topics; or just two people listening to each other masturbate.

Pornography or porn – in its broadest state, it is the explicit representation of the human body or sexual activity with the goal of sexual arousal and/or sexual relief. It is similar to erotica, which is the use of sexually-arousing imagery for artistic purposes.

Red-oil (also known as Palm-oil) – a form of edible vegetable oil obtained from the fruit of the oil palm tree. Previously, it was the second-most widely produced edible oil after soybean oil.

The Xhosa – people who are speakers of Bantu languages

that live in south-east South Africa and, in the last two centuries, throughout the southern and central-southern parts of the country.

The Zulu – a South African ethnic group, consisting of an estimated 17-22 million people who live mainly in the province of KwaZulu-Natal, South Africa.

(All definitions are derived from www.wikipedia.org)

STD Resource Info:

Where can I get more information?

Division of STD Prevention (DSTDP)
Centers for Disease Control and Prevention
www.cdc.gov/std

Order Publication Online at www.cdc.gov/std/pub

CDC-INFO Contact Center
1-800-CDC-INFO (1-800-232-4636)
Email: cdcinfo@cdc.gov
Website: www.cdc.gov

CDC National Prevention Information Network (NPIN)
P.O. Box 6003
Rockville, MD 20849-6003
1-800-458-5231
1-888-282-7681 Fax
1-800-243-7012 TTY
E-mail: info@cdcnpin.org

American Social Health Association (ASHA)
P. O. Box 13827
Research Triangle Park, NC 27709-3827
1-800-783-9877

www.ingramcontent.com/pod-product-compliance
Lightning Source LLC
Chambersburg PA
CBHW061652040426
42446CB00010B/1700